≈ ≈ ≈

CAMILLE, 1969

≋ ≋ ≋

Camille · 1969

HISTORIES OF A HURRICANE

Mark M. Smith

Mercer University Lamar Memorial Lectures No. 51

The University of Georgia Press   Athens and London

© 2011 by the University of Georgia Press

Athens, Georgia 30602

www.ugapress.org

All rights reserved

Designed by Mindy Basinger Hill

Set in by 10.25/15 Calluna

Printed digitally in the United States of America

Library of Congress Cataloging-in-Publication Data

Smith, Mark M. (Mark Michael), 1968–

Camille, 1969 : histories of a hurricane / Mark M. Smith.

    p.   cm. — (Mercer University Lamar memorial lec-
tures ; no. 51)

  Includes bibliographical references and index.

ISBN 978-0-8203-3722-7

1. Hurricane Camille, 1969. 2. Hurricane Camille,
1969—Historiography. 3. Senses and sensation—Mississippi—Gulf Coast—History—20th century. 4. Gulf Coast
(Miss.)—History—20th century. 5. Gulf Coast (Miss.)—
Social conditions—20th century. 6. Gulf Coast (Miss.)—
Race relations—History—20th century. 7. Hurricanes—
Social aspects—Mississippi—Gulf Coast—History—
20th century. 8. Natural disasters—Social aspects—
Mississippi—Gulf Coast—History—20th century.
9. Disaster relief—Mississippi—Gulf Coast—History—
20th century. I. Title.

F347.G9S64 2011

363.34'922—dc22   2010045384

British Library Cataloging-in-Publication Data available

FOR RAEGAN, my shelter in the storm

≈ ≈ ≈

Contents

≈ ≈ ≈

Illustrations

≈ ≈ ≈

Preface

When Dr. Sarah Gardner invited me to deliver the Lamar Memorial Lectures at Mercer University in October 2009, I was deeply flattered. The lectures are—quite rightly—recognized as the most important lecture series on southern history and literature in the United States. I follow in the footsteps of some exceptional scholars, including Cleanth Brooks, Bertram Wyatt-Brown, James C. Cobb, Donald Davidson, Drew Gilpin Faust, Barbara Fields, Trudier Harris, Eugene Genovese, Jack Greene, Jack Temple Kirby, and Michael O'Brien, among others. For that reason alone, I had to ponder whether to accept the invitation. I paused for another reason: did I have anything new or original to say? My answer was yes, I did; but, oddly, what I have to say is on a topic and a time that I know relatively little about. My topic is about a place (southern Mississippi) far removed from my English roots and positioned in a time—1969—at which point in my own life I was a year old. I am, by training, a historian of the antebellum South, of slavery, of economics, in the main, and most of my published work has been on those subjects. In the past decade, my work has expanded to include an interest in the history of the senses—how sight, sound, smell, taste, and touch—functioned in the past, especially in the nineteenth-century South. But as I pondered the Lamar invitation, I realized that I had, in fact, nothing terribly enlightening to say about the nineteenth-century South and slavery—certainly not three lectures worth. Why? Mainly because I'm deeply involved in a project funded by the National Science Foundation (NSF) that has led me to a very particular time and place that is—superficially at least—far removed from the history of antebellum slavery.

That project concerns recovery trajectories from natural disasters generally, from Hurricane Katrina specifically, and involves especially an understanding of Hurricane Camille, which hit southern Mississippi in August 1969. The NSF grant is a significant one because it involves large questions and engages several scholars. It is led by geographers at the University of South Carolina and includes a statistician, an expert in gender studies, and yours truly, a historian.

The multiyear grant is designed to examine differential recovery rates resulting from Hurricane Katrina in southern Mississippi. As part of that examination, I was invited to provide some historical context (i.e., to show what the historical record says about recovery from hurricanes in the South). In addition to surveying the dozens of hurricanes that hit the region over the past three centuries, I opted to examine a hurricane that was similar to Katrina both in terms of path taken and extent of damage. Unlike Katrina, Camille is a hurricane that has received relatively little scholarly historical treatment, even though the historical record is quite full and empirically robust.[1]

In the Lamar lectures, I offered three lectures on a particular event delivered by a historian who doesn't often venture into twentieth-century southern history and from a member of an interdisciplinary team that is still collecting and collating its data. We do not yet know all the answers, and the history of Camille is still in the process of being told. I could easily have chosen safer grounds for the lectures.

But I decided to offer three lectures on Camille for good, historical reasons. In the informed but speculative spirit of the Lamar lectures, I present empirically grounded meditations on a topic that has implications for our understanding of the past as well as policy in the future.

I have framed the lectures—and, subsequently, this book— around three topics. The first topic—and the subject of chapter 1—revolves around how the history of Hurricane Camille can grant us access to much larger questions concerning the nature of human experience, that is, the ways in and by which we process and define meaning. This chapter explores the history of the senses, which is a relatively new historical route of inquiry, along with the history of natural disasters. It does so in an effort not only to capture something of the human experience of living through the most powerful of hurricanes but also to suggest something particular about southern history and its fragile, ambivalent relationship with modernity and how that experience is processed in multivalent, deeply textured ways.

Chapter 2 shows that although Camille was removed in time from the antebellum South, the region's history was critical to shaping short- and long-term reactions to the storm. It examines the role played by race in the reception and management of Camille, and it is enlightening for a multitude of reasons—not the least of which is that the storm, while certainly a "natural" disaster, like any hurricane, was also a disaster that hit a particular place at a particular time, with a particular history. That specificity tells us a great deal about the way natural disasters have to be fully contextualized and historicized if they are to be understood properly. If Camille is the story of a hurricane hitting southern Mississippi, it is also the story of a hurricane hitting historically produced and specific forms of local and national social, political, and economic relations, ones that ended up weaving the short-term recovery from a natural disaster into the long-term, man-made disaster of racial injustice and inequality.

Chapter 3 explores whether Camille, specifically with regard to the political economy and recovery strategies used to address the hurricane's aftermath, bequeaths us any enduring lessons about how and how not to enact recovery plans. In an attempt to frame this question and gesture toward an answer, I delve into the meanings that different constituencies attached to the idea of recovery after Camille, explore the structural mechanisms that were (and were not) in place to foster the multiple, and often competing, definitions of recovery, and then examine how recovery—more appropriately understood as a process of "recovering"—played out among different constituencies and groups. Again, I stress the preeminent importance of context produced by past experiences and anticipated futures in shaping differential recovery experiences in southern Mississippi—not only in the immediate aftermath of the storm but also for years to come.

It is tempting to offer extended comparisons between Camille and Katrina, and to a limited extent, in this last chapter, I do. But those more sustained comparisons are available elsewhere. Rather, it is my aim to excavate the histories of Camille, to give them due attention, and to shed light on a hurricane that has not received nearly as much popular or scholarly attention as Katrina.[2]

ಌ ಌ ಌ

Acknowledgments

First and foremost, I wish to offer a hearty thank you to Mercer University's Lamar Memorial Lectures Committee for the extraordinarily kind and deeply flattering invitation to deliver the 2009 Lamar lectures. Committee members and Mercer faculty members made my visit memorable and extremely pleasant. My sincere thanks to the committee members—Nancy Anderson, Mike Cass, David Davis, Sarah Gardner, Tom Scott, Hugh Ruppersburg, Andrew Silver, and Doug Thompson—for giving me the opportunity to present my work. President of Mercer Dr. William D. Underwood and Provost Wallace Daniel were extremely gracious in their hospitality. They have my sincere gratitude. Bobbie Shipley organized things with impressive precision. My thanks to all.

This book is the product of an unwitting public/private partnership. The Lamar lectures are made possible by a generous bequest from Eugenia Dorothy Blount Lamar. I hope this book does some justice to the Lamar family's generosity. This book is also possible because of a National Science Foundation Grant (CMMI-0623991). This grant was awarded to a group of scholars at the University of South Carolina to better understand the nature of differential recovery after Hurricane Katrina in southern Mississippi. My role in that project, as the historian of the group, was to provide some context for understanding the way that recovery from hurricanes in the past—including Camille—might shed light on the region's experience with Katrina. My opinions, findings, and conclusions or recommendations expressed in this material are mine alone and do not necessarily reflect the views of the National Science Foundation or my fellow researchers. I do, though, wish to thank my fellow NSF researchers, Professor Susan Cutter (the grant's principal investigator), Professors Jerry Mitchell, Lynn Weber, and Chris Emrich for their immensely helpful guidance. I have benefited from many of our discussions.

Also, my thanks to both Robert Brinkmeyer and Kent Germany, colleagues who helped guide me on some important matters. Their suggestions were very helpful.

I'm especially indebted to Ehren Foley, one of my doctoral students at the University of South Carolina, who provided simply invaluable help with much of the research. I hope he knows how grateful I am. My sincere thanks to Christian Pinnen who helped me locate the images used in the book. My thanks also to Derek Krissoff and Jon Davies at the University of Georgia Press for working with me on the book's publication, as well as to Claudia Gravier Frigo for her stellar copyediting and to David Prior for preparing the index.

I tested ideas that constitute chapter 2 at the Disaster Roundtable Workshop 21, sponsored by the National Academy of Sciences (Keck Center, Washington, D.C.), on October 17, 2007, and I learned a great deal about recovery trajectories from disasters on that occasion.

≈ ≈ ≈

CAMILLE, 1969

> Man is affirmed in the objective world not
> only in the act of thinking, but with *all* his senses.
>
> KARL MARX, Economic and Philosophic Manuscripts of 1844

ॐ ॐ ॐ

CHAPTER ONE The Sensory History of a Natural Disaster

Official metrics of Category Five hurricanes—maximum sustained winds of at least 155 miles an hour, barometric pressure below 920 millibars, and a storm surge of eighteen or more feet—don't quite capture the raw power of the phenomenon. The sheer intensity is hard to convey. Big hurricanes, such as Camille, provide enough energy in a few hours' time sufficient to supply the United States with a year's worth of electricity; the atomic bomb dropped on Hiroshima was measured in millitons but the energy from Category Five hurricanes is measured best in thousands of *megatons*; the winds of a Category Five hurricane, and the sand they whip into a frenzy, strip not just clothes off people, but they can also blast away the very skin.[1] Such is the power and devastation wrought by these most powerful of hurricanes that the word "storm" seems inappropriate, weak, and oddly quaint to describe them. Such hurricanes are, quite simply, almost unimaginably strong, thoroughly indiscriminate, and unapologetically ferocious.

Category Five hurricanes that make landfall are unusually rare. In the twentieth century, before 1969, only the 1935 Labor Day hurricane had done so. Camille was, at the time, the only Atlantic hurricane with officially recorded sustained wind speeds of 190 miles per hour until 1980's Hurricane Allen. It had the distinction of being the only Atlantic hurricane to make landfall at or above such intensity. Camille's official peak storm surge was a staggering twenty-four feet.[2]

Camille landed around midnight on August 17, 1969, and devoured the coast of southern Mississippi with appalling appetite. It began on August 5, off the west coast of Africa, and lumbered nearly due westward, becoming identifiable on satellite imagery by August 9. Camille teased meteorologists by feinting toward Florida initially and caught them by surprise by tracking northwest directly into Mississippi's Gulf Coast, tumbling into the mouth of the Mississippi River. Camille weakened quickly as it progressed inland. Within twelve hours of moving ashore, it was reduced to a tropical storm.

Camille was also a southern hurricane, hugging some of the geographic borders of the old Confederacy. On August 20, the remnants of Camille turned eastward through Kentucky and dropped heavy rainfall in West Virginia and Virginia, saturating already wet soil and causing massive, destructive landslides. Later that day it barreled into the Atlantic, regained strength, and then was finally absorbed by a cold front.

Camille was dead by August 20, and so were at least 131 people in Mississippi; almost 9,000 people were injured. In total, Camille caused at least $1.42 billion in damages (estimates in 2005 dollars range up to $11 billion): 5,662 homes were destroyed, and 13,915 homes experienced major damage. Up to that point, Camille was the second-most expensive hurricane in the United States (behind Hurricane Betsy). Camille—and the hundred or so tornadoes that it birthed—raked a massive swath of southern Mississippi, hitting Waveland, Biloxi, Pass Christian, and Bay St. Louis especially hard.[3]

2 *Camille, 1969*

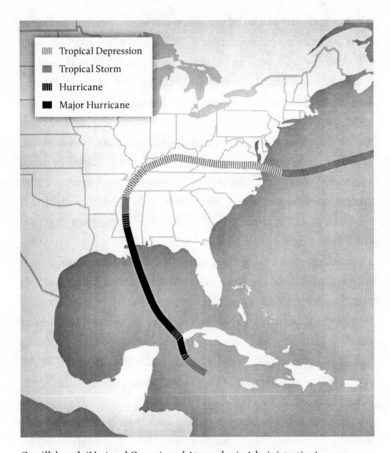

Camille's path (National Oceanic and Atmospheric Administration).

That is Camille in bald, statistical terms. I want to add the human dimension to the hurricane. What was it like to experience Camille? I will excavate the experiential dimensions of Camille in a new way, by attending to the full sensory impact the hurricane had on people, social structures, and behavior. What were the sights of the event? What did it look like both during and after Camille landed? What were the sounds and the smells of Camille, short and long term? How did Camille affect the senses of touch and taste? What can those sensory experiences tell us about Mississippi in 1969 and about the nature of the South generally? If we listen carefully to the words of survivors, it becomes clear that the sensory experience of Hurricane Camille was, for its victims, an atavism—a moment that reminded them that despite their progress and their apparent mastery of modernity, they were, in fact, fragile creatures. For many, the sensory experience of Camille represented a throwback, no matter how temporary, to a sort of sensory premodernity. Twentieth-century Americans generally held a conviction that they had done much to master the world, sensorially and otherwise. Barely three months before Camille hit, Americans landed on the moon and claimed space as their new frontier. And Mississippians, replete with their own local John C. Stennis National Aeronautics and Space Administration (NASA) center located in Hancock County in southern Mississippi, were as buoyed as anyone else.

Mississippians were also convinced, as moderns generally were, that they had gone a long way toward mastering the sensory world, regulating many sights, sounds, smells, tastes, and touches. In this respect, they were not unusual. One of the many metrics of modernity in the Western world used by people to gauge the nature of their "progress" was the extent to which they had come to exercise control over their environment, and central to that understanding was the way in which they believed they had contained, shaped, manipulated, and relied on their senses and sensory environments.

Hurricane Camille exposed the conviction that the senses were at once reliable and controllable as an empty conceit. Sight, once considered so reliable and assumed to be the arbiter of truth and knowledge, was now tested; sounds, once controlled by noise ordinances and architecture, now proved fugitive and beyond control; smells and stench, once contained underground or managed through refrigeration, erupted with nostril-filling force; key social protocols concerning touch—who could touch whom and how, especially in a racially segregated society—applied only in part; tastes once unimaginable to a U.S. palate now had unprecedented currency. As one reporter put it in 1947, a hurricane can throw civilization "back a couple of centuries in less than two hours."[4]

Such claims are bold and warrant some explanation. Moreover, because I am dealing with a relatively understudied way of examining historical experiences, before we consider the sensory history of Hurricane Camille, I think it helpful to discuss briefly the nature of historical work on the senses and their supposed relationship to modernity.

In the past couple of decades, what some historians refer to as "the history of the senses," or more simply "sensory history," has burgeoned. Judging by the proliferation of books, articles, journals, book series, and especially conferences on the history of the senses in the past decade, we are in the midst of a sensory scholarly turn. Scholars from an impressive range of disciplines, including historians, now process the sensory worlds of the past imaginatively and with increasing authority. The questions they pose are as varied as the answers they offer: What role did smell and olfaction play in eighteenth- and nineteenth-century France? How did olfaction inflect religious values and practices in medieval Europe and under classical antiquity? What role did street-lighting play in nineteenth-century London, America, Chile, and Russia? How did tactility, touch, and hapticity generally inform emerging protocols of political democracy? What role did gustatory and aesthetic taste play in the evolution of national identity? How did the senses underwrite histories of race, class, and gender? How did protocols of listening and hearing inform histories of technology, urbanization, and industrialization?

In posing and answering these and many other questions, historians of the senses have tended to trace the evolution of a particular sense, although recently some have begun to call for greater emphasis on intersensoriality—that is, on how the senses worked together to shape meaning. Broadly, sensory history tends to consider not only the history of a given sense but also its social and cultural construction. Further, it deals with the way that people thought about the senses, the cognitive processing of their sense perceptions, and takes seriously the full social and cultural context of those experiences. Critically, sensory history, as a field, methodology, and scholarly habit, is careful not to assume that the senses are some sort of "natural" endowment but, rather, insists on locating their meaning and function in specific historical contexts. Above all, sensory history is most properly conceived of as a *habit*, a way of thinking about the past, and a way of becoming attuned to the wealth of sensory evidence embedded in any number of, ironically enough, visual texts.

Interpretively, although sensory history is helpful for explaining what people experienced in the past, for adding texture to those experiences, and for showing what people sensed generally beyond just seeing, it also speaks to larger questions concerning when and how different societies moved from premodernity to modernity. Conventional wisdom argued that the combination of the print revolution and the Enlightenment in the West initiated a revolution in the senses, shifting sensory ratios so that sight became elevated, increasingly associated with knowledge and truth, and the lower, proximate senses were denigrated, relegated to the margins. In this interpretation, smell, taste, touch, and, to a lesser extent, sound were far less important to elaborations of modernity than sight, which supposedly became the preeminently authenticating sense in the modern world.

In several important respects, as I have argued elsewhere, the prevailing association characterizing the so-called proximate senses of smell, taste, and touch as "premodern" is misleading and cloaks the ways in which nonvisual senses proved central to the elaboration of modernity in a number of societies, especially in the West but also in other areas of the world during and after the nineteenth century. By the same token, in modernity, sight was not always stable, rational, or true. It could be misleading or disrupted, and it was not always a wholly reliable source of knowledge and truth. Although I do not deny that the print revolution and its attendant developments certainly empowered vision in some important ways, I maintain that it did so quite unevenly and certainly not always at the expense of the other senses. The proximate senses of touch, taste, and smell retained enormous currency during and after the Enlightenment, inflecting modernity in important ways. Trying to frame the shift from premodernity to modernity in terms of a rearranged sensory hierarchy conceals a great deal, in particular the ways in which all of the senses retained authenticating power for all moderns. Smell, touch, taste, and hearing, as well as vision, all functioned in certain contexts as sources of reliable knowledge, of truth, and as part and parcel of the modern age. The point I wish to stress in this chapter—and one that can only be made if we qualify the conventional argument regarding modernity and the senses—is that natural disasters generally and Hurricane Camille in particular destabilized all of the senses, thereby calling into question southerners' relationship with modernity. All of the senses worked to underwrite the modern period, and Camille served to undermine them all.[5]

The sights, as seen in the photographs on pages 8–11—improbable, idiosyncratic, and counterintuitive—were brutally disturbing.

TOP Boat in yard, Biloxi, Mississippi (National Oceanic and Atmospheric Administration Central Library). BOTTOM LEFT The Kimbus House, Bay St. Louis, Mississippi, replete with hurricane proof carport and stone wall, before Camille (Photo from the Bob Hubbard Camille Photographs, McCain Library and Archives, University of Southern Mississippi). BOTTOM RIGHT The Kimbus House after Camille (Photo from the Bob Hubbard Camille Photographs, McCain Library and Archives, University of Southern Mississippi).

Main Street, Pass Christian, Mississippi (Photo by Fred Hutchins, the Hurricane Camille Photograph Collection, McCain Library and Archives, University of Southern Mississippi).

Rubble buried sand along Gulfport's beaches; seawalls, formerly so massive and impregnable, were now fissured and fatigued; ships surrendered to the sea and anchored in high ground; once manicured lawns, proud and resplendent, were now gouged and misshapen; trees and chunks of brick peppered withered tarmac roadways; skylines, once punctuated by slanted roofs and vertical walls, now revealed the flat horizon, one complimented by foundation slabs so scourged by the hurricane that even the plumbing systems had vanished, root-canalled from the concrete; dead bodies, bloated and beaten, peppered Biloxi Beach; and television sets, dozens of them, littered the seashore, plucked by a 24-foot wall of water and 190-mile-per-hour winds from a TV repair shop. These were the visual signatures of the aftermath of Hurricane Camille.[6]

Camille landed at night, and as such, the hurricane challenged vision, making optics horribly spastic. First, the storm rendered what had been within human power to lighten—the darkness—dark once again, returning Camille's victims and survivors to a preelectric age. Eyes accustomed to seeing nighttime contours were challenged, and sight's orbit was limited to just a few feet. People lay in ditches throughout the night and could see only when natural light emerged. The lucky ones—if that's the right word—caught fleeting glimpses of their rearranged landscapes, courtesy of flashlights, before dawn revealed the devastation.[7]

Sunlight itself brought only new, strange, disturbing sights. Gone was the orderliness of linear vision, a sort of seeing anchored by geometric streets, planned buildings, vertical walls, and familiar spaces. Straight roads were rendered disjointed, their smooth lines shattered by fallen trees. The sheer scale of the destruction

Ships heaved ashore, Gulfport, Mississippi (National Oceanic and Atmospheric Administration Central Library).

OPPOSITE TOP Beachfront Drive, Bay St. Louis, Mississippi (National Oceanic and Atmospheric Administration Central Library). OPPOSITE BOTTOM Long Beach, Mississippi (Photo by Fred Hutchins, the Hurricane Camille Photograph Collection, McCain Library and Archives, University of Southern Mississippi).

was "incomparable" to anything even survivors of other hurricanes "had seen before."[8]

Pass Christian's police chief, Gerald Peralta, captured the visuality of rearranged space succinctly: "Everything that was down on the beach was gone. It was all piled up on Scenic Drive, and so on, and so forth." Former landmarks—sturdy landmarks seemingly anchored forever—had vanished. "When I got to Pass High School, then I seen the church, the rectory, and all this was gone." Visual catastrophe invited grammatical confusion. "You know, there just wasn't nothing there." Vietnam was his only real reference: "The closest thing I can associate this thing with is Vietnam. The way it's leveled after a bombing. This is the closest thing."[9]

Vision, reliable vision, the sense that moderns everywhere had come to believe (hence the phrase "seeing is believing"), was also destabilized by the debris or, rather, what the debris hid. Lumber and trees, once secured material, now hid sights that modern eyes were relatively unaccustomed to seeing. As one witness recalled: "You didn't know whether there was a body under it or not." Eight days after Camille, a man's body was seen "on top of a tree where the water left him when it went down, with a mattress on top of him."[10]

Those were the sights of immediate aftermath, but Camille had others in store, ones that lasted for weeks. Debris hid bodies—limbs braided with wood, splinters, and metal. These sights were accessible only through glances, too painful for prolonged staring. Small towns, such as those hit by Camille, were often close knit and recognizing a dead body's familiar face, often disfigured by water and weeks of heat, proved hard. Police chief Peralta recalled of a friend: "What it was, one of them big cranes had picked up debris, and her arm fell out. . . . I couldn't, I didn't want to look that close, but I recognized the dress because it was a dress that she used to wear quite a bit." The two or three days following Camille "were the most hot and humid days I'd ever seen in my

life. I mean it was hot." Bodies decomposed rapidly; skins black-
ened—"[b]lack and blue completely"; their bodies were "beat up"
not just by the pounding of bobbing or grazing but by the August
Mississippi heat that spanned into September and October.[11]

And then the sightseers came—literally wishing to see what
they had never seen—to test the reliability of their eyes. The police chief recalled, "But the biggest problem after the hurricane
was your sightseers." They interrupted progress and made residents feel ghoulish, their destroyed lives on display for those who
wanted to feast their eyes.[12]

Not everyone wanted to see the carnage. Some residents moved
inland after Camille not only to render themselves less vulnerable
but also to shield themselves from sights that triggered memories.
"I like it better here for one reason," recalled one survivor a decade
after Camille: "here you cannot see no signs of Camille. . . . On
the west end, you'll see broken trees, dead trees, a lot of empty
lots and everything. There's too much memories of the hurricane
over there. And here you can forget it easier, you know, more than
when you're back there."[13]

Neither temporal distance from Camille nor prior experience with
hurricanes dulled the senses. Ten years after Camille, Lee Roy
Clark Jr., who had been through the powerful New England hurricane of 1938, couldn't shake the sensory experience of Camille
because it was at once thoroughly multisensory and profoundly
atavistic. Camille's sound was "the weirdest sound I have ever
heard in my life," he noted; it reminded him of "Ghosts." It was
"an odd, whine-like sound. I mean, I don't ever want to hear that
sound again." The sound of Camille, then, was something beyond
historical comprehension for Clark, his only operational acoustic metaphor something fantastic, immeasurable, supernatural,
beyond grasp.[14]

Yet it was the long-term auditory signature of the event that lingered most powerfully with people, not just the immediate sound of Camille rushing in with ferocious noise and pounding water. One survivor offered the telling observation that years after the event, those who had experienced Camille and those who hadn't—those who were relative newcomers to the area—could be spotted easily: "And if you ever wanted to find out who had been in Camille, or who knows anything about Camille, buy you a chain saw and start it up, and watch the expressions on their face, and you can tell who's been in Camille. That's one noise people will never forget. It would start at five in the morning, and then they'd go to about seven at night." He reflected: "I can be anywhere now, and a chain saw will start up, and I'll stop. It's just that you heard it for months, and months, and months, nothing but chain saw. That's how you can tell who's been in Camille." He concluded on a touching note: "Now the wife, if you start a chain saw, the wife will get tears in her eyes, because we'd lay in bed and listen to them."[15]

For some people the memory of long-term recovery sounds, although important, couldn't compete with the sounds the night Camille hit. "I've heard other people say that the thing they remember the most was the sound of chain saws," mused Clark's interviewer, "because they heard them every daylight hour for the next three months, just constantly." Clark agreed but added acoustic layers: "Yes, chain saws. Oh yes, day after day, night after night, they'd start off." But there was more to it: "But the transformers blowing up, and the howling, that strange howl."[16] Camille disrupted the soundscape of southern Mississippi in profound ways, ripping through modern efforts to modulate it, refine it, and control it through ordinances and architecture—the same tools we use today—and leaving lasting impressions years after the event.[17]

Camille also suspended, rearranged, and challenged the senses of taste and smell for many residents. Like other places in the modern United States, pre-Camille southern Mississippi was a place that for over a century had benefited from and deployed certain technologies, such as sewer systems and refrigeration, to contain smells and to render food enjoyable and to pander to ever-refined palates.[18] Camille gouged so deeply into southern Mississippi's flat soil that sewage lines were exposed, laid bare, and ruptured, their putrid cargo spewing into the soil. The Gulf Coast's residents had refrigerators, shopping malls, grocery stores, all of which gave them—at least those who could afford it—access to food either fresh or frozen but rarely rancid, unpalatable, or indigestible.[19]

The immediate aftermath of Camille destroyed those technologies and rendered what was once contained and managed now fugitive, roving, and more reminiscent of a presewage, pre-refrigerated past. For example, Camille destroyed the ability to contain stench. Meat, "sides of pork, and this, that, and the other" from restaurants was now strewn about, unrefrigerated, and fetid. "[T]he odors around here was something else," recalled one witness. The memories lasted for years: "strange smelling mud . . . seemed to linger in the air," the aroma easily recalled by residents twenty years after Camille.[20]

Erasing the fetor of Camille's aftermath was also something of a priority of some relief agencies, notably the Red Cross, which went into southern Mississippi shortly after Camille barreled through. Blankets and bedding were, according to one survivor, not dispensed by the Red Cross, at least not immediately. Instead, they gave out "[c]leaning up material. . . . Mops and brooms and stuff." The Red Cross gave others "a pail and a scrub pail with a broom." Cleaning came first, and it was a couple of weeks before "staples" were given out. Here, the association of disease and smell was most likely at play and helps explain the agency's thinking. Even the food that was dispensed by relief organizations held an unusual—and deeply unpleasant—olfactory quality. One survivor recalled being given canned spam. "You open it up, you can't hardly smell it let alone eat it. I mean, you know, I don't have nothing against Spam or nothing, but it just never did smell right." His middle-class palate wasn't used to such tastes, and Camille functioned to rearrange what he wanted to eat and what he had to eat.[21]

Camille, then, exposed tastes taken for granted, returning survivors to palates associated with a premodern time. Yes, those who knew of the storm had anticipated what they called "hurricane food: canned goods and bread and some stuff that didn't spoil" for a few days.[22] But as the extent of the damage became apparent, expectations altered. Water was, in the immediate aftermath, scarce, dispensed weekly by the National Guard from a truck. Thirst, the absence of liquid on tongues accustomed to easy quenching, was a feeling horrible in its novelty. The taste and feeling of cold on tongue was a cherished experience in the aftermath of Camille, especially given the necessity of performing hard, manual labor in hot weather. For some, the Salvation Army became associated with "cold drinks," Gatorade most notably.[23]

Camille intervened into a place and a moment where the protocols governing the senses of touch and hapticity mattered a great deal. Mississippi, like everywhere else, had particular rules concerning touching and skin. Some of these protocols were broadly American: skin was supposed to be clear and uninfected, courtesy of a multimillion-dollar skin-care industry. Skin was also meant to be cared for, covered against the elements, and protected. Camille mocked those cultural conceits.[24]

For example, in the moment of the hurricane itself, wind and rain beat skin, treating it with a contempt few had experienced. Clark recalled that he "was beat up, yes, when that rain and stuff hit." It was the "cold and wet," that feeling of absented modern comfort—the skin exposed and raw—that lingered with him and many others. People craved clothes that were "clean" and "dry," their skin unaccustomed to bone-grinding damp, matted clothing. The false respite brought by the eye of the hurricane invited a different tactile experience. For Clark, not only was the eye "still," the absence of wind and rain a haptic relief, but it also made his skin feel "sticky-like." Sticky. Unwashable. The sweat of desperation mingling with the feel of incredibly low pressure.[25]

Camille's passing left scars, literally—dead bodies riven, welted, marked, histories of debris scratching, slamming, and scraping written into their skin.[26] And for the living, scars from infections and surgery served as visual and haptic reminders of the damage done to bodies for years.[27]

Then there were rules of touch that, although not wholly particular to Mississippi, were certainly pronounced there. These were the protocols governing racialized touch. Black people, unless invited, were not supposed to touch white skin. Black men especially were not allowed to touch white women, and history was a fair guide to the consequences for those who did.[28]

Camille suspended those protocols. Mary Ann Gerlach's encounter with Camille was one mediated largely through the skin, at least as she distilled it in her memory of the event. Pain, touch, and race figured prominently. Gerlach—middle class, white, and female—was hit hard by Camille, her "bleeding and skinned up" body draped over a pile of debris. Unable to move, she begged for help from equally dazed passersby. A slightly built man—about 135 pounds—named Frank, whom she knew from the post office, heard her cries and came over. "Mary Ann, is that you?" he asked. Frank's eyes betrayed him because Mary Ann's body had been exposed by Camille. In addition, as Mary Ann explained, Frank had "never seen me without my wigs on, or my hair done up, and all my make up." Her visual public self was unrecognizable to Frank, who had only the sound of her voice to go on. Hearing trumped seeing. Frank struggled with Mary Ann, who weighed as much as he did, carrying her "a little ways," then putting her down to regain his strength, as he tried to get her to the nearest hospital.

Frank's shoulders were tired, and he must have been pleased when he saw his "six foot five" postal office coworker. He was black. For Frank to transfer Mary Ann to the coworker, cultural norms concerning the touch between a black man and white woman had to be suspended. Frank asked Mary Ann, "Would you mind if this colored man carried you up to the road where we could get an ambulance or something?" She agreed, and "he picked me up in his arms like a little baby." In the immediate aftermath of the terrible storm, decades-old rules were suspended.[29]

Others agreed. "Everybody you met" in the immediate aftermath of the storm "you hugged them, whether it was man or woman. I remember the old gardener, the old colored gardener, when he came in he just threw his arms around me."[30]

In some ways, of course, it makes little sense to segregate the senses in the way I have done. To talk just of the auditory, tactile, gustatory, visual, or olfactory experience of Camille seems contrived, framed around and in the service of scholarly, interpretive conceits, without true fidelity to the multisensory experience of Camille. Although treating the sensory experience of Camille discretely is indeed illustrative and conceptually helpful for understanding the precise ways in which people encountered the storm, fundamentally, Camille was a thoroughly multisensory, intersensorial event whereby the senses operated interactively. For example, Camille stole modernity's sensory prosthetics. "I was bare-footed, I lost my shoes, my eyeglasses," recalled one man, his customarily protected feet now forced to touch materials ordinarily never in contact with his soles, his eyes now forced to squint and see in new ways.[31]

Sound and touch frequently coincided, understandably because vibrations are heard through feeling. Camille "was the most horrible sound, and I have never forgotten it," recalled one woman a decade after landfall. "If we start to get any kind of storm here," she mused, "I can hear it. I can hear it coming. It really is tremendous. It's not wind as much as it is pressure. . . . It's so strong, the vibrations. . . . the vibrations in your ears." For others, the winds "were real noisy," not unlike the sound made by "freight trains" throwing "on their brakes with a bunch of cargo." Like the noise of Camille's wind, the brakes "whine when you put them on." "And it stayed with me. . . . Like a train that passed a long time ago, and it's still going on in the distance. You know they go rickety-rickety over the tracks. I can hear that."[32] Trains are felt and heard all at once, like Camille, vibrations generating feeling as well as sound.

Others couldn't decide on the principal sensory signature of Camille, wrestling between sight and touch. "If you'll think back about Camille right now," ventured his interviewer, "is there anything that really stands out in your mind[?]" Clark struggled. "The force," he answered. "The force and the blackness." He elaborated: "The blackness, and just the tremendous force of it. And the water, it was, I mean it was just like you turned a faucet on, and the wind force of it, that water hitting [you] in the face." Sight and touch braided for Clark, the blackness of not seeing constituted by the force of stinging water and rain not allowing him to see.[33]

What best sense can we make of this sensorial treatment of Camille? At the most general level, a sensory history of Camille grants us some admittedly tentative access to the South's fragile and conditional relationship with modernity. Because hurricanes hit the southern United States more than they do any other region of the country and because the embrace of modernity has been more tepid in the South, a sensibility that is arguably more of a southern mentality than anywhere else in the nation, we cannot but wonder whether the two are connected. If a region that experiences hurricanes disproportionately also struggles with its relationship to modernity more than any other part of the country, perhaps there is a connection between the two, one mediated by the senses—mediated by a profound experience in which assumptions about the reliability and mastery of the sensory world are routinely shattered by the power of nature, a power so great that those sensory conceits and confidences are not only exposed but also rendered more akin to assumptions about the senses in the premodern world than they are in the modern world.[34] In other words, if modernity is, in part at least, understood in terms of the regulation and attempt to control the senses, it is an aspect of modernity frequently embarrassed by the power of nature's most ferocious storms. That that embarrassment happens with greater frequency in the U.S. South might explain why the region's culture has struggled to place unwavering faith in the modern condition and all of the elements of control that that condition seems to promise. Perhaps in this way, the South's tenaciously ambivalent relationship with modernity, at least in the twentieth century, makes sense.

20 *Camille, 1969*

Never let a serious crisis go to waste. What I mean by that
is it's an opportunity to do things you couldn't do before.

RAHM EMANUEL, White House Chief of Staff, November, 2008.

ૠ ૐ ૐ

CHAPTER TWO **Desegregating Camille**

CIVIL RIGHTS, DISASTER RIGHTS

I begin this chapter by contradicting the first. I begin, also, with a
quotation. The quotation is from the *Congressional Globe*, March
29, 1867. We join Charles Sumner of Massachusetts on the floor
of the U.S. Senate as he offers an amendment to a bill providing
federal relief for broken levees in Mississippi. Keep in mind the
year and context: 1867, in the cauldron of Reconstruction.

> I am unwilling that Congress should seem in any way to com-
> mit itself to so very great an expenditure in one of these States,
> except with the distinct understanding that it shall not be until
> after the restoration of the State to the Union on those principles
> without which the State will not be loyal or republican. We are
> all seeking to found governments in these rebel States truly loyal
> and truly republican. Will any such State be truly loyal or truly
> republican until it has secured in its constitution the elective
> franchise to all, and until it has opened free schools to all? . . .
> A State which does not give the elective franchise to all without
> distinction of color is not republican in form, and it cannot be
> sanctioned as such by the Congress of the United States. Now

I am anxious, so far as I can, to take a bond in advance, and to hold out every temptation, every lure, every seduction to these people to tread the right path; in other words, to tread the path of republicanism and loyalty. Therefore I seize the present occasion to let them know in advance that if they expect this powerful intervention of Congress they must qualify themselves to receive it by giving the evidence that they are truly republican and truly loyal. . . . It is an immense charity, a benefaction, from which private individuals are to gain to a great extent. Thus far these levees have always been built, as I understand—I am open to correction—by private individuals, by the owners of the lands, and by the States. . . .

. . . Now, it is proposed for the first time that the national Government shall come forward with its powerful aid. Are you ready to embark in that undertaking? I do not say that you should not, for I am one who has never hesitated, and I do not mean hereafter to hesitate, in an appropriation for the good of any part of the country if I can see that it is in any respect constitutional. . . . I mean always to be generous in my interpretations of the Constitution and in appropriations for any such object; but I do submit that Congress shall not in any respect pledge itself to so great an undertaking, involving such a lavish expenditure of money, except on the fundamental condition that the States where that money is to be invested shall be republican in form and truly loyal; and I insist that not one of those States can be republican or truly loyal except on the conditions stated in my amendment.[1]

The amendment was as follows:

Provided, That it is understood in advance that no appropriations for the levees of the Mississippi river shall be made in any State until after the restoration of such State to the Union, with the elective franchise and free schools, without distinction of race or color.

Camille and segregation (photographer unknown).

What Sumner was saying was simple: Want federal funding? Change your social and political institutions. The relevance of Sumner's speech will become apparent.

Now for my qualified contradiction to chapter 1. In that chapter I stressed the value of all of the senses, especially the nonvisual senses, in capturing some of the texture of the event. Here, I present, in purely visual form, an image capturing the thesis of this chapter: race, and the history that underwrote the idea, was nestled deep in the debris of Camille.

We have come to think of natural disasters as just that: disasters shaped by the hands of nature, their timing and point of entry into our world, as insurance companies tell us, an act of God. And there are good reasons for this way of thinking, this way of framing, this way of managing. Natural disasters are, after all, just that at some level. We can no more control the timing or the placing of a hurricane, an earthquake, or a tornado than we can control the setting of the sun. We are to some extent mere observers of the event, mere custodians of the moment of observation, and in that sense, the event is one that acts *upon* us. For all of our scholarly talk about human agency, natural disasters, in their raw form, challenge our sense of control. Yet we must be careful not to be lulled into thinking ourselves helpless creatures. Camille's wreckage, as awful as it was, must be understood as a natural disaster that barreled into, and cobbled onto, a man-made one: the disaster of race relations in southern Mississippi, a disaster with a history equally replete with dead bodies, withered edifices, flattened horizons, and disturbing sights. It was not a coincidence that when Camille made landfall, a group of Justice Department lawyers were huddled in a Biloxi hotel room, braving the storm, even as they "continued to work right through the hurricane" preparing a school desegregation case they were scheduled to deliver in court three days later, on August 21. In many respects, the story I want to tell is about that apparent coincidence, about the intimate connections between the most powerful hurricane in U.S. history and the country's efforts to come to terms with three centuries of racial injustice, and about the ways in which disaster relief and civil rights were actively interwoven by particular federal officials.[2]

Context, as always, matters. At the national level—one which, as we'll see, became important to local issues—the United States had a new president, Richard Nixon. Nixon's carefully crafted "southern strategy" was designed to appeal to conservative white southerners, who traditionally voted Democratic but who were deeply disaffected by Lyndon Johnson's support for the civil rights movement. Nixon attempted to wean these southern white conservatives from the Democratic Party by emphasizing themes of law and order and, importantly for our purposes, states' rights. Mississippi itself was still a profoundly segregated society with marked racial inequalities. Nowhere was this more evident than in the state's public education system. Ironically, Mississippi's public education system was originally biracial—born during Reconstruction, when newly emancipated slaves lobbied effectively for a system of public education. However, beginning at the turn of the twentieth century Mississippi and the nation began to retreat generally from the lofty ideals of Reconstruction and embraced, instead, jim crow segregation. As a whole, Mississippi's education was mediocre for whites and wretched for blacks, but the former remained wedded to it for the simple reason that the system allowed for all-white schools. So invested were white Mississippians in the system that by 1969, the promise of *Brown v. Board of Education*, mandated fifteen years earlier, was still largely unfulfilled and ignored. Despite a history of activism among the region's African American leadership, despite the hard work of black community leaders, such as Biloxi NAACP chairman, Gilbert Mason, and notwithstanding some limited desegregation in Harrison County in particular, it seems fair to say that by the time Camille hit, not only were schools still segregated but they were also very much unequal. A State Department of Education report in 1962 put the disparity into graphic relief: The average school district in Mississippi spent an average of four dollars on every white child and one dollar on every black one. Over half of the state's 638 black schools remained unaccredited mainly because of awful facilities and horrendous teaching loads. One black school's library comprised six incomplete encyclopedia sets and a dictionary; many of the classes had sixty or more students. This pitiful system was underwritten by tenacious white efforts to allow little more than "token school integration" and equalization of school facilities.[3]

Unsurprisingly then, from beginning to end, Camille was thoroughly politicized. Even as local and state officials engaged in the hurricane recovery, they debated, often fiercely, not only school desegregation but also the way hurricane relief and civil rights had been linked by federal officials. Juxtaposed with—and inextricable to—newspaper reports about the enormous damage caused by the storm were discussions concerning desegregation, the rights of local authorities, the role of the federal government in enacting integration, and curiously enough, the Nixon administration's determination to establish a new antiballistic missile defense system.[4] In short, any understanding of Camille as a natural disaster must be read in the larger historical and social contexts of southern and U.S. history.

Ted Steinberg has argued that natural disasters in U.S. history have tended to become so reified and have been treated in such a discrete fashion, a fashion that artificially segregates the disaster in question from its larger social and historical context, that our response to those disasters "often winds up justifying and thereby preserving a particular set of social relations." Careful attention to the context of Camille, however, shows how some federal officials deliberately attempted to integrate the disaster and its social context. By insisting on the complementary nature of civil rights and disaster relief, federal officials and bureaucrats treated disaster relief in a holistic fashion, articulating—and actively interweaving—immediate concerns over hurricane relief and recovery with pressing questions about long-term social injustice.[5]

Even before Camille made landfall, segregation and old southern protocols governing "racial etiquette" were at play. I'll not dwell on this issue here because, courtesy of a very long and detailed set of Congressional hearings conducted in 1970, the facts are well known and, to my mind, incontrovertible. Suffice to say, black and white perceptions of how Mississippi's population was handled during Camille could not have been more different. Black complaints about the treatment of evacuees stood in stark contrast to an often self-congratulatory emphasis among white officials about the importance of "community-sharing" in preparing for Camille, a trope of community cooperation that has infested a great deal of the historical memory about Camille.[6] African Americans, by contrast, argued that segregation, not community cooperation, had guided the process of evacuation in advance of Camille's landfall. They pointed out, for example, that they were sent to the "Negro Jackson State College" and that "Negroes were not welcome at the evacuee center set up in the old Robert E. Lee Hotel" in Jackson. Initially, even the evacuation buses were segregated. In the face of an imminent, devastating natural disaster, southern Mississippi's commitment to segregation dictated evacuation procedures with a tenacity not unlike Camille's most uncompromising winds. Although white Mississippi officials, including Governor John Bell Williams, denied the charges, race and segregation were inextricably linked to Camille—before, during, and after the storm.[7]

Long- and short-term historical patterns governed a great deal of what happened. The hurricane landed in a context in which the desegregation of Mississippi's schools was part of the public discourse. Plans to implement school desegregation in all of Mississippi's school districts had been on the books for some time. Harrison County, for example, one of the counties most affected by Camille, had planned to achieve integration by transferring 250 North Gulfport High School students to the Harrison County High School in the autumn of 1969. By January of that year, a timetable was in place, and the local school board appeared to be in compliance with a court-backed U.S. Department of Health, Education, and Welfare (HEW) stipulation that the schools integrate by or on August 11, 1969.[8]

Meanwhile, some powerful national forces were working to postpone school integration, not just in Mississippi but also throughout the South. According to Lee Bandy, writing for the Washington Bureau of the *Biloxi-Gulfport Daily Herald*, eleven days before Camille made landfall, the South's chances for resisting school desegregation were "brighter than usual" because "the Nixon administration," which had assumed office on January 20, 1969, was "quietly supporting" an amendment inserted into a HEW appropriations bill by Democratic house representative Jamie L. Whitten of Mississippi. Whitten's measure was designed "to legitimize freedom-of-choice plans" and, critically, to "prevent cutoff of federal funds to noncomplying school districts." Behind the scenes, Nixon staffers rallied House members behind the Whitten provision. Thus, it had become quite clear that the Nixon administration not only viewed the question of school desegregation through a highly political lens but also construed the original phrase of the 1954 *Brown* decision, with "all deliberate speed," as a license to treat school desegregation lethargically.[9] At the time, though, the Senate had yet to vote on the measure and was, in Bandy's estimation, likely to block it, just as it had stymied similar legislation a year earlier.[10]

Camille barreled into this debate and, courtesy of some key federal officials, became connected to the question of school desegregation. On Tuesday, August 26, 1969, nine days after the storm's landfall, Guy H. Clark, chief of field operations for the U.S. Office of Education, told forty or so Mississippi administrators from the schools affected by Camille that "they could expect no federal assistance for repair and replacement of buildings, supplies and equipment if their schools were not in compliance with Title VI of the Civil Rights Act of 1964." Further, no private schools would be aided with federal money, said Clark, attempting to undermine the common southern strategy of sidestepping desegregation orders by establishing white-only private schools. "Only public schools, those in compliance, will be assisted here," maintained Clark.[11] Federal money was meaningful. City schools in Gulfport alone were out of commission for two weeks and about twenty schools were damaged at a cost of one hundred thousand dollars.[12]

What Clark proposed was hardly extravagant. After all, Clark stipulated that "federal help would be limited to no more than that required to reestablish the same educational level that existed before the hurricane," which, in the case of the majority of Mississippi students, black and white, was hardly spectacular.[13] Neither were the mandates of HEW idiosyncratic. Rather, they constituted part of a larger effort by some federal officials in Washington, D.C., not just to effect school desegregation in Mississippi but also to establish some semblance of racial equality. A day after Camille hit, for example, the U.S. Office of Education ordered the state of Mississippi to postpone spending part of a $32.1 million grant from the federal government because federal investigators "had found evidence black students in the state's 149 districts were not receiving an equitable share of state and local money spent for education." This was an early case of the federal government refusing to grant a state monies in order to compel it to allocate its own state and local funding in a manner compatible with federal requirements designed to give blacks "equal education opportunity." The Office of Education's request had been formulated before Camille's landing, but the timing of its announcement was relevant.[14]

White Mississippians reacted quickly. Just three days after Camille made landfall, Mississippi's Association of School Superintendents appealed directly to President Nixon to restore the thirty-two million dollars in federal money earmarked for disadvantaged Mississippi students. Their arguments were revealing. First, they pointed out that 350,000 school children would be adversely affected; second, they argued that without the funding 3,000 faculty and staff in the school system would lose their jobs; third, they felt singled out—Mississippi, they complained, was the only southern state to have its funding suspended by HEW; fourth, they resented the fact that Office of Education officials had bypassed state and local education agencies in their deliberative process; and fifth, they objected that local programs had, courtesy of HEW, been turned over "to a small group of loud dissidents who have no experience in operating school programs."[15]

Nine days after Camille hit, Dr. Garvin Johnston, the state superintendent of education, expressed disappointment specifically with Clark's decision and considered attaching prospective federal disaster relief to school desegregation heavy-handed and illegitimate. Johnston made the case that white schools had been destroyed and would suffer, and he was right. Some schools were beyond recognition. But Johnston was stung by the braiding of civil rights and disaster relief especially: "It's a tragic thing when the government will help only those disaster victims who comply with the administrative edicts of civil rights directives and instructions," he complained. Johnston estimated damage for fifteen Mississippi school districts to be about thirteen million dollars and urged that "all districts apply for help [from HEW] whether they are eligible or not." "Edicts," "directives," and "dissidents"—this was the language of states' rights that had underwritten Mississippi's resistance to school integration since the 1954 *Brown* decision.[16]

Beyond the state, unapologetic political leverage was key to Mississippi's efforts to disentangle federal relief for Camille from school desegregation. Here, we need to consider what was going on at the White House and in the U.S. Senate. When historians have considered Nixon's treatment of Mississippi, they have made a great deal of his position on civil rights and states' rights. As Charles C. Bolton has commented in his excellent book on school desegregation in Mississippi, "Clearly, Nixon was no ardent segregationist. His civil rights credentials dated back to at least the 1960 presidential campaign" when a number of black leaders had endorsed him. Bolton says, further, that Nixon "had no intention of allowing the South to retain segregated schools at this late date." And, concludes Bolton, "[Nixon's] recent political victory at least in part rested on the success of his southern strategy, so he sought to compromise on the pace of school desegregation where possible." Moreover, Nixon did force Mississippi governor Williams to appoint Biloxi NAACP chairman Mason to the all-white Hurricane Emergency Relief Council.[17]

This is all undoubtedly true, but other factors were at work. First among these was the fact that Nixon forced Williams's hand only after Mason and other black activists filed a formal complaint with the Commerce Department, arguing that the council was in violation of Title IV of the 1964 Civil Rights Act that prohibited discrimination in the use and allocation of federal funds. Second was the central importance of Nixon's southern strategy.[18]

Enter Mississippi senator John Stennis, an ardent opponent of integration and also chairman of the Senate Armed Services Committee. Stennis had a great deal to do with Nixon's thinking and, in his opposition to the conjoining of Camille recovery efforts and school desegregation, Stennis, quite literally, went ballistic. When the Nixon administration took office, Melvin Laird, the secretary of defense, suspended an existing deployment program (the Sentinel) and, three months later, announced a new antiballistic missile system, Safeguard. Safeguard was designed to defend intercontinental ballistic missile (ICBM) silos. In May 1972, President Nixon and Soviet secretary general Leonid Brezhnev signed the Anti-Ballistic Missile Treaty and the Strategic Arms Limitation Talks I (SALT) agreement. Stennis had performed invaluable service for the Nixon administration as the floor manager for the Safeguard system, which Nixon had championed beginning in March 1969. At stake was the administration's twenty-billion-dollar weapons' budget. Stennis had "captained the bipartisan forces which gave the administration a breathtaking, one-vote victory for deployment of the Safeguard" system, but now, in early September 1969, he threatened to stop fighting for the important remaining funds in support of the project "unless his repeated requests for a delay in Mississippi school desegregation were heeded." Stennis told Nixon by letter that unless his wishes were granted, he would yield floor management of the Safeguard appropriations bill to Senator Stuart Symington of Missouri, a fierce critic of defense spending.[19]

Stennis's threats fell on listening ears. Nixon's inclination was not to connect disaster relief to desegregation. Vice President Spiro Agnew, per Nixon's instructions, maintained that "the shattered schools would be helped and that matters of desegregation would be attended to later."[20] In fact, according to the NAACP as well as Leon Panetta, director of the Office for Civil Rights, the Nixon administration increasingly embraced the view that desegregation should be slowed down, regardless of Camille, and the administration made its position clear within a couple of weeks of the storm's landfall.[21]

Although not unsympathetic to a slow and deliberate school desegregation policy, Nixon nevertheless found his hand forced and required HEW secretary Robert Finch, who had publicly and steadfastly supported the August deadline regardless of Camille, to move back the date for school desegregation to December 1. Finch, in the unenviable position of contradicting himself at the president's request, had no choice but to agree. The "Mississippi school desegregation mystery," as it was referred to by contemporaries, was no mystery at all. Simply put, because of Stennis's threats and because the Nixon administration was determined to fully fund the Safeguard system—and not because of Camille—HEW was forced to postpone the date for school integration in Mississippi, moving it from August 11 to December 1, 1969. But Stennis's critical role here was muted both by the press and by HEW, which now argued that the real reason for deferring the desegregation date was due to the "chaos" that would result from trying to desegregate in the context of the destruction wrought by Camille.[22]

Whatever the public statements, Finch's stance did "not reflect the position of the Nixon administration." Agnew said as much, although according to the *New York Times*, in a comment of curious prescience, "[t]he accounts of precisely what Mr. Agnew said vary, and his press spokesman said the tape cartridge on which the Vice President's remarks were recorded was 'jammed'" and, therefore, could not be verified. The appalling irony of a missing "fragment" from Agnew's comments, courtesy of a "broken tape" notwithstanding, Agnew was "more than mildly annoyed" by Clark's statement and considered efforts to interject questions of desegregation into disaster relief unwelcome and inappropriate. Yet even under pressure from the White House, HEW and the Department of Justice initially stuck to their guns by insisting that the two issues remain fused. "We are going to try to arrange a plan to integrate," said a representative of the Office of Civil Rights, "[t]hat will make them [sixteen of the states' school districts] eligible for disaster assistance."[23]

What is most revealing about this episode, however, is that Stennis got relatively little for his efforts—merely a four-month deferment (a sliver in the African American experience with racial injustice). This is not to minimize those four months; rather, it is to stress that HEW had so braided Camille with desegregation that Mississippi's most powerful senator was forced to resort to relatively drastic, transparent, and heavy-handed measures to get what amounted to very little. As the actions of forty attorneys in the Justice Department's Civil Rights Division, who threatened to resign over Stennis's strong-arm tactics, and the NAACP, which roundly criticized the Nixon administration, reveal, HEW's authority was, in some respects, more than a match for Stennis who could only postpone the implementation, not prevent it. Part of the issue here stems from Finch's rather awkward position vis-à-vis the Nixon administration. He appears to have been required to toe a line that favored court-enforced decisions rather than the HEW initiative. Finch used HEW's (threatened) power over funding to accelerate desegregation quite publicly and, for this reason perhaps, earned the support of some black leaders who thought him well meaning but hostage, in part, to the Nixon administration's larger indifference toward school desegregation. Critically—and this is my central point—by tying Camille to civil rights, HEW had effectively shone a light on the centrality of desegregation.[24]

HEW, Finch, and Panetta did not give up. In mid-November, HEW, backed by the courts, reiterated its threat to withhold funding, a threat that still had enormous currency because of the destruction wrought by Camille (and a threat that would have had fewer teeth without Camille). HEW understood this leverage and kept pressing, continuing to pair hurricane recovery with desegregation in an effort to mandate the new, December 31 deadline for Mississippi school integration. But there was a price to pay: the White House forced Panetta to resign on February 18, 1970, precisely over the desegregation issue. Nixon, according to the *New York Times*, had caved into Stennis. Finch and HEW were, as a result, left increasingly isolated, attempting to enforce a policy the Nixon administration found anathema.[25]

The history of Hurricane Camille cannot reliably be read outside of its context. That context spanned three centuries and had everything to do with a genealogy of endemic racial injustice. The history of Hurricane Camille helps revise common wisdom about the function, nature, and imaginative capacity of federal officials and bureaucrats. Now largely a synonym for sluggish, unimaginative, and hidebound policy making and behavior, federal bureaucrats, at least those in the Office of Civil Rights and HEW, responded to a natural disaster courageously and promptly and with an expanded sense of their official capacity to initiate social change. Here, I take strong issue with Nathan Glazer's bad-tempered characterization of HEW and, especially, of Panetta's handling of Camille. Glazer writes: "In his bureaucratic rigor, Panetta even denied nonconforming Southern school districts relief aid in the wake of Hurricane Camille, despite the intervention of Vice-President Agnew. There is much to be learned from this fascinating account about how one ideological and narrow-minded bureaucrat may stalemate an administration." To the contrary, the Panetta-HEW response was far from narrow-minded; rather, it suggests the capacity of the bureaucratic mind to forge creative and substantive solutions that attack short- and long-term social problems simultaneously.[26]

Camille tells a story of a federal bureaucracy that did not segregate a natural disaster from its social context. Instead, the activities of HEW—and officials such as Panetta and Finch—suggest the power of the bureaucratic imagination. Such activities also demonstrate the willingness of certain officials to merge artificially discrete topics to institute a more ecumenical "recovery" and thus, in the process, to redefine the relationship between social justice and federal relief. The redoubtable Senator Sumner from Massachusetts understood this only too well in 1867. The question remains, Why was Sumner's understanding largely forgotten until Camille, and why has it seemingly been forgotten since?

we will learn along the way what to re-use,
what to throw away. we will make mistakes
and try again, hoping to get it right, because
this is what we do: in the face of destruction
we clear the debris and rebuild it—
whether we should or not

KATE GREEN, "Reconstruction," 2006

ॡ ॡ ॡ

CHAPTER THREE The Political
Economy of Disaster Recovery

By any measure, the economic cost of Hurricane Camille was staggering. Over six thousand destitute families were counted in September alone; the hotels, businesses, and homes that once populated the eighty-mile length of the Gulf Coast where Camille slammed ashore "lay flattened." Two towns in particular, Pass Christian and Long Beach, had been "virtually blown away from the face of the earth." Early, rough estimates were staggering: over two hundred dead, twelve thousand homes destroyed or very severely damaged, and six hundred businesses gone. About one-third of Mississippi's economy had vanished.[1]

In this chapter, the questions I wish to ask and go some way toward answering are as follows: How did Mississippians recover in the short and long term? What were the mechanisms for economic recovery? What role did local and federal authorities play in that short- and long-term recovery? And most important, did those efforts work? The answers to these questions serve as powerful reminders that we would be unwise to use the term "recovery" broadly. Recovery, its speed and meaning, was radically different for varying constituencies. And the reasons for those different results and varying trajectories have everything to do with the specificity of historical context—and politics especially.

Recovery from anything, especially a natural disaster, is a slippery term, laden with politics. Recovery implies completion, a return to a predisaster condition. In that sense, it is not unlike the word "reconstruction," yet we know full well that instances of reconstruction in U.S. history are hardly that. Perhaps the gerund—recovering—is more apt because it correctly implies a process, one not anchored by linear trajectory or fitting a scripted blueprint. But it is an inelegant word, even though I think it a more accurate one. And so when I use "recovery," I really mean "recovering" because, in the case of Hurricane Camille, the place never recovered in the literal sense of the term, at least not for all the constituencies involved. In short, recovering from Camille was very much a tale of two Mississippis, and these two stories are best told by examining recovery in both the short and long term. The initial impact of Hurricane Camille tended not to discriminate. Everyone who was hit was hit hard. But later, as days merged into weeks and months, it wasn't the hurricane that differentiated; it was the various responding relief agencies that made politically motivated decisions about where to allocate relief funds and introduced the discriminatory wedges that had long-term impact.

From the very beginning, Camille was a source of utter confusion. Many people heard nothing about the impending storm. "[W]e didn't hear or see anything that was going on with regard to this Camille thing," remembered one resident. Those without radios or televisions heard nothing and were woefully underprepared. Even those with radios heard little. As a result, many people did not evacuate or did so at the last minute.[2] Further, there was not a great deal of information for those who dragged themselves out of battered homes the next day. "Most people had no idea what aid was available, where to get it or how to get there (most cars and buses were battered, too)," recalled a survivor.[3]

Everyone muddled through, at least in the first days. People gathered and searched for belongings, raided soda machines, shared clothes, erected makeshift shelters. Private enterprise did the same. One local bank manager explained: "The immediate impact of Camille on the banking industry on the coast was that it shut it down. The banks that were still there, that didn't have any water damage or hurricane damage, were able to operate. But for a few days, you couldn't get a cash letter in. You couldn't get one out. You couldn't get a telephone call out of town." Within forty-eight hours, though, banking operations were beginning to return to something resembling normal.[4]

Early options, even for short-term recovery, were few and largely unsatisfactory. Insurance offered little in the way of private stimulus for recovery—which is, after all, one way insurance can be conceived.[5] Individual stories, of which there were thousands, stand as proxy for a general trend. Take Herman W. Ryals, a retired civil service worker. His modest frame house, near the beach at Gulfport, Mississippi, was destroyed by Camille. He and his wife were still living in a trailer four months later. Judging by the insurance settlement they received, that was to be their future: the company paid only 25 percent of his claim. Ryals sued; the outcome was unclear. But many others found that they could not rebuild.[6]

The evidence suggests that coastal residents, even affluent ones, were wholly underinsured. Majestic columns couldn't be replaced—the cost of new ones was prohibitive; less expensive substitutes were used in rebuilding—and sheet rock often replaced the original plaster in walls. Other residents found that many insurance policies failed to cover particular items. Jewelry looted in the immediate aftermath of Camille wasn't covered, and only wind damage—not water damage—was paid for. One woman from Waveland recalled, with impressive precision, what insurance did and didn't cover a decade after Camille: insurance paid for "anything connected with the greenhouse, the boathouse, the two shops that were there, the bicycle shop. . . . Those were damaged minutely, you know, little things. . . . . But he did not pay for any water damage whatever. Just wind damage." Such was "the typical story."[7]

But the problem wasn't simply one of underinsurance. The reluctance of insurance companies to pay up what they in fact owed resulted in a grand jury investigation. Moreover, shortly after Camille, Mississippi's insurance commission approved a 50 percent rate increase for the coast. According to one report: "[I]nsurance adjusters descended in droves, pressuring wiped out families in desperate need of money to settle for a quick cash settlement worth only a fraction of their total damage claims."[8]

There were other sources of help, however. Alexis de Tocqueville, that most astute of observers of the American national character, believed that a principal signature of that character was voluntary associations. And if Camille is any measure, he was partly right. Private voluntary associations came to help, and quickly at that. The Salvation Army was apparently on the scene almost immediately in some areas.[9]

Many of the hurricane victims ended up going to the Red Cross, that renowned quasi-governmental agency, chartered by Congress as "America's official human relief organization" while retaining control over its finances and operations. The organization's self-proclaimed mandate: helping families "resume their normal family life in the home and in the community" following natural or man-made disasters. Although they gave grants and not loans for food, housing, and clothing, the Red Cross, according to Biloxi NAACP chairman Gilbert Mason, "told people to exhaust all other possibilities for aid before coming to them."[10] Moreover, the organization's mission statement was inherently biased toward the already comfortably off: "The poor get just enough to restore their shacks, the middle class receive much bigger grants to re-build their comfortable homes." One reporter cited an example in which "a $39,000 income family received a full bedroom outfit, while another family, which made $3,000 per year, got a mattress." The same policy applied across the board and included food with moderate-cost plans going to the middle class and lower-cost ones that place "a heavier reliance on less expensive food groups, such as potatoes, legumes . . . flour and cereals" being allocated to poorer families. African Americans were especially critical of the organization. Mason said: "[T]he most dehumanizing, deni-grating, humiliating and bureaucratic demon to appear on the Gulf Coast after Hurricane Camille is the American Red Cross." Black memories of the Red Cross's documented discrimination against African American flood victims, dating back to the 1920s and 1930s, were also at work here.[11]

From the perspective of middle-class business leaders, though, the very presence of the Red Cross and other relief organiza-tions in southern Mississippi after Camille functioned as a mini-economic stimulus. Quick to arrive on the scene, Red Cross of-ficials "came in and began buying from the local stores: beds, fur-niture, replacement items for people who had lost everything." A local bank manager recalled, "[W]hat they were doing was generat-ing business at a time when the stores were in desperate need of it." The practice helped pump "some money into circulation" and functioned as "a normal business cycle but magnified down into a disaster area."[12]

Survivors ranked the relief agencies. A local police chief thought the Salvation Army superior to the Red Cross; the lat-ter he considered stingy, rationing items. But the Salvation Army, "they never would tell you no." A Waveland woman was also criti-cal of the Red Cross that "gave me a mattress, box springs," and "that was all." Well, not quite: "Oh, and a box of Kleenex." But

the Kleenex lasted long enough to help her get through an or-
deal with the next federal agency: "Now the Kleenex I received
where we had to wait to see the man about our property" was
used to dab the sweat from her forehead—and also, perhaps, to
wipe away the tears. "[A]ll we could get was a mattress and a box
spring."[13]

Others applauded both the Red Cross but especially the Salvation Army for providing food and drink when it mattered: "They
were right there with food and cold drinks when we were trying
to do this work in the hot sun. A truck [from the Salvation Army]
went around every hour with Gatorade and things like that, you
know, that you really needed when you were trying to get the
things done."[14]

On the whole, these relief agencies and the people who staffed
them seemed too overwhelmed by the extent of the damage to
offer anything more than light triage.

More substantive, and more geared toward longer-term recovery,
was federal relief. Key here was Housing and Urban Development
(HUD). Victims went to HUD field offices to apply for trailers. A few
of the agency's temporary trailers—home to some people for a
year—arrived quite quickly after the storm, some as early as late
August. But getting one could be challenging. HUD regulations
were quite stringent, class biased (and in the context of Mississippi, race biased), and difficult for many people to understand.
For example, families whose lots were small or who could not
clear debris did not qualify for HUD assistance. Some families
whose houses had been severely damaged and rendered unlivable
could not afford to demolish what was left of the property and
encountered difficulty in getting HUD assistance.[15]

Moreover, that HUD provided trailers was not apparently widely
known, and the agency ended up extending the application period by a month. Even if families qualified, trailers were scarce.

The majority of trailers did not arrive in the affected areas until November. By late October, only sixteen trailers had made it to the hard-hit inland regions. And even those families who navigated the eligibility hurdle and then secured a trailer ended up signing blank leases with HUD. "HUD simply hadn't formulated its terms," and many families had no idea how long they could stay or how much they would pay. Only at the end of October did HUD issue guidelines on these matters: the agency would pay the fifty-dollars-per-month rent and utilities for three months. After that, families would have to pay, even though the law permitted the government to pay up to a year. The trailers weren't cheap either. As one Camille survivor recalled, simply: "There was heavy rent for them."[16]

If HUD couldn't help, the next stop for Camille's survivors was the Small Business Administration (SBA). Survivors seemed no happier with this federal agency. The SBA received a lot of criticism, in fact. Some SBA administrators, for example, demanded full financial disclosure before they would commit the SBA's financial assistance. "No," recalled one woman after an SBA interview, "I'm not going to tell you every nickel that I have. Besides that, you want me to tell you every penny that I have, and then what to do with it." The SBA official replied: "Well, just go on home and use it all. And when you have no more left, then come back and see us." The woman had better luck in the private sector: the Ramada Inn in Waveland "gave us milk and food."[17]

To be fair, many survivors did receive meaningful recovery assistance from the SBA. The SBA did loan money to families to buy plots of land on which to build new houses.[18] But the SBA loans were a lasting curse for many. A study on the psychological effects of Camille conducted three years after the storm suggests that roughly ten months later, once life began to resume something of a regular meter, some survivors showed signs of long-term depression, a condition indexed to that moment when "the burden of paying off heavy SBA loans began to be felt as the burdensome reality that they are."[19]

On the whole, in the eyes of the average survivor, as ineffective as some voluntary relief agencies were, federal ones were worse. One survivor was even critical of the Corps of Engineers. Overall the Army Corps of Engineering "did a good job," doing "eighty or ninety percent good," notwithstanding the Corps's temporary workers, "outsiders," who, many residents believed, "didn't know what they were doing." But in its zeal to get rid of debris, the Corps sometimes removed precious earth from housing sites, requiring residents to buy soil and dirt to provide the new houses with higher and level foundations.[20] More generally, the Army Corps of Engineers also compromised the economic recovery effort for businesses: during its clearing of the debris it elected to issue twenty-one million dollars in contracts to out-of-state firms instead of local ones. Asked about the contacts, the Corps maintained that the bids from Mississippi firms were too high. Its spokesman added: "We can't give them preferential treatment."[21]

In some relief, Camille exposed preexisting inequalities among large groups. For example, age was an important variable in affecting individual recovery. For some elderly, Camille, at least in family lore, functioned as a "stress" trigger, initiating long-term physical decline. So too in the immediate aftermath of the storm when the "older people" in hospital were markedly "tired, depressed, and lonely."[22]

Camille hit, as we have seen, within a particular context and at a particular moment, a moment when race was arguably the region's principal social signature. As such, relief efforts were often framed and articulated within that particular idiom. Take, for example, the way the Mississippi State Bar Association used a fifty-thousand-dollar Office of Economic Opportunity grant, awarded in late August, to help with a legal service program for victims of Camille. None of the money, as far as we can tell, ended up assisting those most in need of it. Instead the president of the bar, Boyce Holleman, the district attorney who zealously prosecuted civil rights workers in 1963–65, appears to have directed the money toward white, predominantly lower-middle-class families. Furthermore, as the Combined Community Organizations Disaster Committee (CCODC), a group dedicated to advocating for poor and black Mississippians in the wake of Camille, argued: "The Mississippi state bar has placed barriers in the path of out of state, ie. civil rights lawyers, from offering free legal advice to hurricane victims. Not even during an unprecedent[ed] natural disaster is the racist state bar association prepared to alter their legal monopoly."[23]

In some ways, initial relief efforts and recovery trajectories placed class and, especially, race differences into clear profile, which the habits of day-to-day life can sometimes mask. Take, for example, evidence concerning epidemiology. Although we have less direct data for southern Mississippi, we do have quite detailed information regarding morbidity rates in the hurricane shelters for Plaquemines Parish, Louisiana, which was also hit by Camille. Shelters, as in Mississippi, were segregated, although the degree of overcrowding in white and black shelters was roughly the same. There, similarities between black and white ended. "Whites appeared to be more actively engaged in recovery of losses, through salvage operations or hasty insurance claims. . . . It was not unusual, during the first two weeks, to find blacks who had not yet visited their damaged properties." At least a couple of factors were probably at work here: African Americans, courtesy of lower levels of automobile ownership, were less able to visit their homes in the days following Camille, and they had fewer insured homes or belongings worth salvaging. Epidemiological and medical consequences followed: "Skin and wound infections in blacks occurred at about twice the rate of that in the white population," probably because they engaged in "somewhat more frantic salvage operations" once they could organize access to their properties.[24]

African Americans certainly perceived that they were the victims of both the hurricane and institutional racism. Biloxi NAACP chairman Gilbert Mason charged that HUD, the SBA, and the Red Cross discriminated against African Americans in their allocation of emergency relief, noting that these agencies tended to dedicate disproportional resources to projects favored by the white business community—industry, golf courses, marinas—rather than toward the poor and most recovery-challenged. Thanks to the efforts of Mason, state NAACP president Aaron Henry, the CCODC, and Robert Clark—the only black representative in the state legislature and Chairman of the CCODC—Mason, and a handful of other African Americans, were given a voice on Governor John Bell Williams's formerly all white Hurricane Emergency Relief Council. But these additions to the Council were not made until January 1970 and the bulk of the emergency relief still went to business.[25]

Class—itself inextricable to race in this context—also mattered a great deal. Those with money and social clout attempted to parley it in the immediate aftermath of the storm. Mary Ann Gerlach didn't want to stay in the Miramar Nursing Home—it was filthy and without much by way of medical facilities. She wanted to go to the Keesler medical facility, one deemed better and less damaged by the storm. She told the ambulance driver: "I've got a little money in the bank . . . and what I don't have, I've got friends, got some family and I'll get the money." She got there.[26]

Members of the region's white middle class considered themselves disproportionately affected by the storm. "I think probably that the middle class got it in the neck again," mused banker John Switzer. He explained: "[A] hurricane strikes and damages the area that is the highest cost per square foot of land, the beach front, the waterfront." Because "higher priced homes are built in those areas," if the property wasn't insured, both the middle class and "the upper class too" were especially affected, in Switzer's opinion. There was more than a whiff of class consciousness in Switzer's evaluation of the differential impact of Camille. Yes, "I was able to qualify for a SBA loan," as were many of his customers, "but had to pay competitive market rates for it." He had little sympathy for the more economically challenged: "These people, if they were hurt, were hurt because they simply chose to spend the money that they had for something else rather than buy insurance."[27]

For those without resources, the hurricane and the relief policies underwriting recovery arguably helped create a new class of poor in southern Mississippi. Five months after Camille, it was clear that this new class existed. There were forty-nine hundred families still homeless in January 1970. These were erstwhile working-class families who now lived in emergency HUD trailers, fretted over how to pay their bills, worried that their HUD leases were about to expire, agonized about how to buy food, and remained largely unemployed. To be sure, in early 1970 the Department of Labor released eight hundred thousand dollars in Emergency Disaster Unemployment Compensation to Mississippi workers, but it wasn't enough, not least because local industry was still struggling to recover itself, let alone employ large numbers of people.[28]

The poor were also penalized by SBA procedures and protocols. Once in their HUD trailers, families and individuals could apply to local SBA officials in an attempt to secure financing to rebuild their homes. The process was cumbersome for two reasons. First, SBA officers were as affected by Camille as everyone else and, in the immediate aftermath, hardly functional. One Office of Economic Opportunity (OEO) official told of "finding a man wandering the streets mumbling about the SBA. I asked him

if he needed help finding their office, and he said, 'Yes, I'm the local SBA representative.'" Second, SBA rules and regulations favored
those with collateral. According to one report, "The poor had no
collateral, and middle- and marginal-income families who once
had collateral had lost it to Hurricane Camille." As a result, most
loan agencies automatically discriminated against the poor and
therefore against blacks—particularly the SBA, which "granted
over 90 percent of its loan dollars to whites." The relatively few
loans issued by the SBA to African Americans was, then, about both
race and class. The SBA loan applications were very detailed and
challenging for the poorly educated. The SBA was less than helpful in such circumstances. Said one SBA official: "We don't have
much patience with someone who can't fill out a form." The SBA
sometimes referred such people to lawyers, some of whom charged
up to two hundred dollars to complete the application.[29]

Camille affected workers across the board, of course, but some
occupations were harder hit than others. Measured in unemployment claims—for which we have reliable records—we can see a
fairly predictable pattern. For the remaining two weeks of August after Camille hit, claims for 32,545 weeks of unemployment
were filed. For September, the claims dropped to 27,643 weeks;
for October, only 18,366 weeks were filed. This initial rapid drop
reflected the allocation of labor to the recovery effort. Many of
those whose conventional jobs had vanished were now enlisted
in cleanup and recovery projects as well as in construction crews.
By November, though, unemployment started to increase, mainly
because money for cleanup projects was running out and because
previously existing businesses were not yet operational. This was
especially true of manufacturing and the hotel industry, which,
combined, accounted for 55 percent of all unemployment claims.
Another reason for the increase in unemployment claims was due
to Camille's disruption of agriculture in the area, especially in
tung-nut harvesting. Most of the tung-nut trees were destroyed

by the hurricane. Unemployment continued to increase until February 1970. In terms of race, white men tended to find work more quickly than black, although both received similar levels of state unemployment. Because agriculture and manufacturing were hardest hit and because they employed most poor whites and blacks, Camille can be said to have had a differential effect on the recovery of southern Mississippi residents according to class.[30]

Perhaps the most important factor in shaping who got to recover and how was politics. The particular configuration and structuring of state, federal, and municipal authority in the aftermath of the hurricane did much to further marginalize the poorest members of southern Mississippi and checked their recovery rate relative to that of the middle class. The principal reason for this differential in recovery has to do with the authority invested in the governor's office by the Nixon administration when it came to the dispersal of federal relief funds.

The federal agency charged with—and arguably most sympathetic to—dealing with what was termed "social rehabilitation," assisting the poor especially, was the Office of Economic Opportunity, an agency created in 1964 as part of President Lyndon Johnson's Great Society program. Within three weeks of Camille hitting, the OEO had functioned as a model of efficiency by visiting the other federal agencies involved in the relief effort and drafting a series of detailed recommendations for each. For example, the OEO established blueprints for day-care education (thus allowing parents of young children to find work), transportation pools (essential, given the scarcity of reliable motor transportation), and special outreach programs for the elderly. According to one OEO official, the agencies ignored them. "All the agencies told us the poor are OEO's problem," he said. That responsibility in itself, while a staggering one, would perhaps have been a more manageable one had the OEO had access to significant funds. But it didn't. The reason is straightforward.[31]

On September 6, Mississippi governor Williams formed a twelve-member Governor's Emergency Council (GEC), seeded by a half-million-dollar grant from the Commerce Department's Economic Development Administration. Its aim was to draft a plan for the region's long-term economic recovery: "President Nixon designated the GEC as the single contact point for all Federal aid." According to a detailed report published in the *New Republic* in January 1970, the council became the clearinghouse and recipient for significant federal funds. The *New Republic* was hardly surprised that "[i]n a state which is 43 percent black, and largely impoverished, Williams appointed to the Council ten white, rich bankers, realtors, attorneys and corporative executives." On September 16, President Nixon issued an order requiring "all agencies and departments of the government of the United States . . . to coordinate their activities" via the council. As a result, the council oversaw the spending of $100 million in federal aid (that's a little over $600 million today). This is not to say that the council had fiduciary power over all expenditures or unbridled political power. We've seen that HEW had enough clout to leverage disaster relief into civil rights. Even so, the council was powerful and had a significant amount of money at its disposal.[32]

As a result, groups out of favor, including the OEO, got very little money from the council. The process of allocating funds was in large part political, playing an important role in how, where, and to whom federal monies—indeed, even private monies—were allocated. The $1.7 million raised by Bob Hope's televised "We Care" fund appeal was apparently used by local government to invest in municipal bonds. Most significantly, though, the governor's council, with its access to a good deal of federal money, opted to make certain kinds of investments. The council allocated funds for some emergency, short-term relief, but the record suggests that the bulk went to investing in what would become today's Mississippi Gulf Coast, what the *New Republic* described as "a $100 million complex with golf courses, boat marines and high-priced apartments."[33]

Why did the Nixon administration grant so much authority to the governor and funnel so much money through the council? There is a case, to be sure, that federal monies are better placed in the hands of local authorities who know local needs, understand the local sociopolitical landscape, and can thereby allocate needed resources most efficiently and precisely. But that, as we have seen, is not what happened. I suspect more crass political motivations were at work. The president helped himself *politically* in selecting the council as the conduit for so much federal money for two reasons. First, doing so probably took some of the sting out of HEW's leveraging of disaster funds and school desegregation. Many white Mississippians had come to accept that public school integration was an inevitable fact of life by 1969 and were probably more miffed at the obvious federal strong arming of the matter by Robert Finch and Leon Panetta than they were at the fact itself. Second, and more important, the Nixon administration made many friends among Mississippi Democrats with its decision to flood the governor's council with the money. In October 1969, just a couple of months after Camille, state Democrats hosted a Republican fund-raiser for Vice President Spiro Agnew, who also toured the disaster area. Fred LaRue, who occupied the odd position of having no official listing in the White House directory but who was an important political aide to Nixon (he would later supervise the shredding of documents relating to the Watergate scandal), understood the importance of the connection. "The indication Nixon wants to do everything possible to help," said LaRue, "is certainly making an impression." For that same reason, and also probably because he was a native of Biloxi, Mississippi, LaRue served as the president's personal liaison with the council. This was simply part and parcel of Nixon's southern strategy designed to bring conservative whites into the Republican fold by stressing states' rights and downplaying any overt or aggressive commitment to civil rights (while, it has to be said, not abandoning the principal cornerstones of civil rights legislation). Precisely because school integration was happening in Mississippi and because Nixon wanted to keep southern Democrats sweet, it made sense for him to make the governor's council the principal custodian of a great deal of federal relief money.[34]

The operative question is this: Did it work? Did the governor's council, with its heavy emphasis on investing in business to aid long-term recovery rather than allocating the bulk of resources for short-term recovery, better help Gulf Coast residents in the end? The question is difficult to answer, not least because a good deal of the available data that we have comes to us from local business bureaus and chambers of commerce who, precisely because they were involved in sponsoring the type of recovery trajectory envisioned by the council, were under some obligation to say that it worked.

The evidence, taken as a whole, from the business community tells a story full of optimism, and not without some basis. Coastal Mississippi, within a few years of Camille, did make something of an impressive comeback, and arguably long-term business investment laid the foundation for the region's later rise as a minitourist mecca replete with casinos and swanky hotels.[35] Certainly, the tourism industry was hit hard by Camille, as hard as any other sector of society. But as devastated as the tourist industry was, it also bounced back quickly and robustly. As early as January 1970, for example, a new six-million-dollar, eight-story, 300-room Sheraton Inn, complete with convention hall, was on its way to completion in Biloxi and was scheduled to open in November of that same year. The 216-room Ramada Inn in Biloxi was even further along: it was scheduled for completion in the spring of 1970.

"Rushing to completion" was a new restaurant and lounge on U.S. Highway 90 in Biloxi, boasting "the finest cuisine with decor to match." New projects were legion. The Pass Christian Yacht Club; new golf courses; a new Motor Inn between Gulfport and Biloxi; Biloxi's Small Craft Harbor, capable of berthing 149 "pleasure and deep sea charter fishing boats"; a shopping center; and dozens of other similar projects were all close to completion less than a year after Camille hit. This wasn't just rhetorical bluster on the part of the business community; this was real, material, observable growth. No wonder people remembered the sound of chainsaws and construction so powerfully.[36]

"From all indications—visible and spoken—tourism appears to have a future as the Coast's and Mississippi's shiniest economic potential," crowed contemporary reports. Or as this assessment put it looking back twenty years: "The storm gave businesses a chance to move, to repair, to modernize." True, but very few private homeowners, especially among the poor, had the resources to modernize their houses in such a fashion.[37]

Other industries also benefited, principally because of the peculiar way this massive experiment in Keynesian economics—the pumping of money into the economy to prime revitalization—was channeled through the governor's council. The council, by most accounts, allocated most money to private businesses, which in turn fueled the growth of others, notably banks. For example, the Hancock Bank had assets of $75 million when Camille rolled through; six months later, the assets had grown to $100 million. The Peoples' Bank of Biloxi experienced similar growth. Its president, Chevis Swetman, reflecting from the vantage point of 1989, said something the vast majority of people who lived through Camille would hear as alien: "We had our best year ever" in 1969. When Camille struck, his bank had one branch, in downtown Biloxi; by 1989 his bank had become one of the state's ten largest, with twelve branches.[38]

Banks. New hotels. Convention centers. Yacht clubs. Pleasure craft harbors. Golf courses. Was this the sort of growth necessary for sustained and equitable recovery? Chambers of commerce, as is their wont, made the trickle-down claim: widespread social recovery, they said, has to be sponsored by business, which in turn will employ people. Yet it should be remembered that in 1969, the hotel industry accounted for only 14 percent of employment in the counties affected by Camille. Moreover, although the building of these new structures certainly employed construction workers, it was likely nowhere near enough to absorb jobs lost or postponed in manufacturing and agriculture. In other words, Mississippi's poor would have been incredulous to hear Swetman call 1969 their "best year ever." This was the recovery divide in operation.

If we define recovery in the same way that the Red Cross did, then it is probable that within a couple of years the poor and per-haps the lower middle class too were no better off—and probably worse off—than they had been prior to Camille. Many businesses, conversely, seemed to have flourished, partly because many had better insurance but mostly because the particular structure of finance recovery allocation through the governor's council, at the behest of the Nixon administration, allowed those in power to select business as arguably the chief beneficiary of recovery funds. Business benefited from Camille and plainly was restored to more than it had been before August 1969, most likely at the expense of the poorer members of southern Mississippi.

My conclusion is really no such thing. It is, really, a historically informed question less about our past and more about our fu-ture. When President Barack Obama visited New Orleans for a few hours in September 2009, he was asked by an unemployed law student, during a town hall meeting, why he, the president, couldn't just write a check to solve what seemed to be the impos-sibly long-lasting echoes of Hurricane Katrina. The question was reasonable: in 2009, more than four thousand survivors of Katrina in southern Mississippi alone were still in search of long-term housing (some of whom were, quite literally, living in the woods), and as with Camille, there have been loud complaints that Mississippi officials have misdirected federal relief funds to rebuilding Mississippi's port infrastructure at the expense of long-term housing for the region's poorer residents.[39] The president demurred, maintaining that he didn't have the authority to write such a check. Technically, of course, the president is correct (although keep in mind that Nixon did, in a sense, write such check in 1969, one made out to the Mississippi governor's council). But perhaps the unemployed student and the president were asking and answering the wrong questions. The operative, pressing question is not so much about writing checks per se; it is more about to whom to write them and the motivation behind such decisions. I cannot say with any certainty that had the Nixon administration allocated the $100 million to other agencies, recovery from Camille would have been more equitable and less marked by a recovery divide. Perhaps money did trickle down from the business community. But even if that is the case, I'm unsure if people who are destitute should be asked to wait for money to trickle in this fashion. Speed is critical. I am rather more certain, however, that motivations matter. If the aim is to effect a speedy, broad-ranging recovery for all citizens affected by a natural disaster, it would seem ethically and morally appropriate for those in positions of political authority to suspend their own political aspirations, worries, and fears, and, put simply, do the "right" thing. History, especially the history of disaster recovery, which recounts how attempts to help disaster victims in the past failed (and succeeded), offers officials at all levels a powerful and quite accurate compass for doing the "right" thing. In the absence of that historically grounded compass, we seem doomed to perpetuate the recovery divide the next time a powerful Atlantic storm decides to cut its teeth on southern soil.

ঽ ঽ ঽ

Notes

PREFACE

1. Although the work that we do have on Camille is generally thoughtful and accessible (written mostly by journalists), it does not discuss many of the topics I raise in the lectures presented here. See especially Stefan Bechtel, *The Roar of the Heavens* (New York: Kensington Publishing Corp., 2006); Ernest Zebrowski and Judith A. Howard, *Category 5: The Story of Camille. Lessons Unlearned from America's Most Violent Hurricane* (Ann Arbor: University of Michigan Press, 2005); Philip D. Hearn, *Hurricane Camille: Monster Storm of the Gulf Coast* (Jackson: University Press of Mississippi, 2004). I have benefited from all three books. In addition to the official records and newspaper articles on Camille, I found the series of oral interviews conducted in the years following the tenth anniversary of Camille by R. Wayne Pyle immensely helpful for capturing the human experience of the storm and its aftermath. These interviews, referred to hereafter as MOI (Mississippi Oral Interviews), are held at the University of Southern Mississippi's Center for Oral History and Cultural Heritage. I have, throughout this short book, attempted to retain something of the flavor of the lectures I delivered while necessarily revising them for publication and all of the stylistic changes that entails.

2. For gestures toward comparisons between Camille and Katrina, see Susan L. Cutter and Mark M. Smith, "Fleeing from the Hurricane's Wrath: Evacuation and the Two Americas," *Environment* 51 (March/ April 2009): 26–36. Work on Katrina is considerable. I found Michael Eric Dyson's *Come Hell or High Water: Hurricane Katrina and the Color of Disaster* (New York: Basic Book, 2006) unusually insightful. See also the excellent collection of essays "Through the Eye of Katrina: The Past as Prologue." *Journal of American History* 94 (December 2007): 693–876.

CHAPTER 1 The Sensory History of a Natural Disaster

1. Comparisons borrowed from Stefan Bechtel's deeply engaging *Roar of the Heavens* (New York: Citadel Press, 2006), 36–38.

2. Bechtel, *Roar of the Heavens*, 38. Reliable statistics are accessible at www.nhc.noaa.gov/HAW2/english/history.shtml#camille.

3. Figures from Philip D. Hearn, *Hurricane Camille: Monster Storm of the Gulf Coast* (Jackson: University Press of Mississippi, 2004), ix, 123; www.harrison.lib.ms.us/library_services/camille.htm (accessed 7/17/2010). See also M. E. Criswell and R. S. Cummins, *Survey of Gulf Coast Structural Damage Resulting from Hurricane Camille, August 1969 Final Report* (Washington, D.C.: Office of Civil Defense, Office of the Secretary of the Army, 1970). My focus here and throughout is on Mississippi, not Virginia, simply because it was the Gulf that experienced the bulk of the damage and because it is southern Mississippi that is the focus of the larger National Science Foundation project.

4. Reporter quoted in Charles L. Sullivan, *Hurricanes of the Mississippi Gulf Coast* (Biloxi, Miss.: Gulf Publishing Co., 1986), 82. On the senses and modernity, see Mark M. Smith, *Sensing the Past: Seeing, Hearing, Smelling, Tasting, and Touching in History* (Berkeley: University of California Press, 2007).

5. These matters are surveyed in some detail in Smith, *Sensing the Past*.

6. "Damage Incredible," *Biloxi-Gulfport Daily Herald*, August 19, 1969; "Victims in Area Listed," *Biloxi-Gulfport Daily Herald*, August 21, 1969; Lee Roy Clark Jr. interview, MOI, vol. 232, p. 37. This chapter

especially relies a good deal on a series of oral interviews conducted in 1979 (and later) of Camille's survivors.

7. Clark interview, MOI, vol. 232, p. 35. On the widespread use of flashlights, see Demetz interview, MOI, vol. 226, p. 41. On the association between light, vision, and modernity, see Smith, *Sensing the Past*, 37–38 esp.; A. Roger Ekirch, *At Day's Close: Night in Times Past* (New York: W. W. Norton, 2005). Neither should this be understood as a short-term effect. For example, immediately after Camille, 100 percent of electricity connections in Harrison County were down; it took fifteen months to restore the county to pre-Camille levels. Kathleen R. Leyden, "Recovery and Reconstruction after Hurricane Camille: Post Storm Hazard Mitigation on the Mississippi Gulf Coast" (Hurricane Hazard Reduction Through Development Management, Report No. 85-15, funded by the National Science Foundation, Grant No. CEE-9217115, August 1985), 40.

8. Clark interview, MOI, vol. 232, pp. 35, 37.

9. Gerald Peralta interview, MOI, vol. 224, p. 36.

10. Clark interview, MOI, vol. 232, p. 36; Gerlach interview, MOI, vol. 178, p. 10.

11. Peralta interview, MOI, vol. 224, pp. 37–38; Jacqueline Fontaine Hines interview, MOI, vol. 230, p. 36.

12. Peralta interview, MOI, vol. 224, p. 38.

13. Mr. and Mrs. Stegenga interview, MOI, vol. 201, p. 52.

14. Clark interview, MOI, vol. 232, p. 35.

15. Peralta interview, MOI, vol. 224, pp. 43, 44.

16. Clark interview, MOI, vol. 232, p. 41.

17. On the modern control of sound and noise, see Emily Thompson, *The Soundscape of Modernity: Architectural Acoustics and the Culture of Listening in America* (Cambridge, Mass.: MIT Press, 2002); Raymond Smilor, "Personal Boundaries in the Urban Environment: The Legal Attack on Noise: 1865–1930," *Environmental Review* 3 (1979): 24–36.

18. On moderns' efforts to manage odor, see Alain Corbin, *The Foul and the Fragrant: Odor and the French Social Imagination*, trans. Miriam Kochan, Roy Porter, and Christopher Prendergast (Cambridge, Mass.: Harvard University Press, 1986); and David S. Barnes, *The*

Great Stink of Paris and the Nineteenth-Century Struggle against Filth and Germs (Baltimore: The Johns Hopkins University Press, 2006). For hints on the U.S. context, see Joel A. Tarr, *The Search for the Ultimate Sink: Urban Pollution in Historical Perspective* (Akron, Ohio: University of Akron Press, 1996); Martin V. Melosi, *The Sanitary City: Environmental Services in Urban America from Colonial Times to the Present* (Pittsburgh: University of Pittsburgh Press, 2008).

19. "In the Wake of Camille," *New Republic*, January 10, 1970, 9. On refrigerators and grocery stores, see Hines interview, MOI, vol. 230, pp. 38, 66–67.

20. Clark interview, MOI, vol. 232, p. 36; Paula Jackson Smith, "A Strange Smell Seemed to Linger," *Biloxi-Gulfport Sun Herald*, August 13, 1989.

21. Clark interview, MOI, vol. 232, p. 39; Edith Byrd De Vries interview, MOI, vol. 201, p. 41.

22. John Switzer interview, MOI, vol. 227, p. 22.

23. Dorothy Mae Demetz Noilet and Fred Demetz interview, MOI, vol. 226, p. 74; Clark interview, MOI, vol. 232, p. 37; Hines interview, MOI, vol. 230, p. 66. Some store owners gave away Cokes and Pepsis. Peralta interview, MOI, vol. 224, p. 40.

24. Along these lines, albeit for earlier periods, a much larger historical arc, and an understanding of skin through multiple lenses, see Virginia Smith, *Clean: A History of Personal Hygiene and Purity* (New York: Oxford University Press, 2007), 224–352 esp.; Suellen Hoy, *Chasing Dirt: The American Pursuit of Cleanliness* (New York: Oxford University Press, 1995), 151–178; Kathleen M. Brown, *Foul Bodies: Cleanliness in Early America* (New Haven: Yale University Press, 2009).

25. Clark interview, MOI, vol. 232, pp. 35, 36. On the need to feel clean and dry clothing, see Switzer interview, MOI, vol. 227, p. 42.

26. Peralta interview, MOI, vol. 224, p. 38.

27. Gerlach interview, MOI, vol. 178, p. 10.

28. On the racialized touch and segregation, see Mark M. Smith, *How Race Is Made: Slavery, Segregation, and the Senses* (Chapel Hill: University of North Carolina Press, 2007).

29. Mary Ann Gerlach interview, MOI, vol. 178, p. 10.

30. De Vries interview, MOI, vol. 201, p. 45.

31. Stegenga interview, MOI, vol. 201, p. 25.

32. Jennie Jenevein interview, MOI, vol. 225, p. 19; Demetz interview, MOI, vol. 226, p. 40. For the sound of the train as an aural signature of modernity, see Mark M. Smith, *Listening to Nineteenth-Century America* (Chapel Hill: University of North Carolina Press, 2001), 44–45, 96, 108, 117, 210, 231.

33. Clark interview, MOI, vol. 232, p. 41.

34. For a sense of just how many hurricanes have hit the Gulf Coast historically, see Sullivan, *Hurricanes of the Mississippi Gulf Coast*. The literature on the South's relationship with modernity is vast, of course, but I still think W. J. Cash's *The Mind of the South* (New York: Alfred A. Knopf, 1941) explores thoughtfully some of the tensions in southern culture, broadly construed, concerning the hesitant embrace of the modern.

CHAPTER 2 Desegregating Camille

Epigraph quoted from "A 40-Year Wish List," *Wall Street Journal*, January, 28, 2009.

1. *Congressional Globe*, 40th Cong., 1st sess., March 29, 1867, 433–35.

2. Quoted from Leon Panetta, *Bring Us Together: The Nixon Team and the Civil Rights Retreat* (Philadelphia: Lippincott, 1971), 253.

3. Charles C. Bolton, *The Hardest Deal of All: The Battle over School Integration in Mississippi, 1870–1980* (Jackson: University Press of Mississippi, 2005), 89–91; Charles C. Bolton, "The Last Stand of Massive Resistance: Mississippi Public School Integration, 1970," *Journal of Mississippi History* 61 (1999): 329–50. On black leadership generally, see John Dittmer, *Local People: The Struggle for Civil Rights in Mississippi* (Urbana: University of Illinois Press, 1994); on Mason, see Gilbert R. Mason with James Patterson Smith, *Beaches, Blood, and Ballots: A Black Doctor's Civil Rights Struggle* (Jackson: University Press of Mississippi, 2000). On Harrison County, see James Michael Butler Jr., "Surface Similarities: A Comparative Analysis of Civil Rights Struggles in Harrison County, Mississippi, and Escambia County, Florida" (PhD diss., University of Mississippi, 2001), 208–22.

4. On the structural links between local, state, and federal authori-

ties in the context of disaster relief, see Ruth Stratton's *Disaster Relief: The Politics of Intergovernmental Relations* (New York: University Press of America, 1989). See also Susan L. Cutter's *Hazards, Vulnerability and Environmental Justice* (London: Earthscan, 2006).

5. Ted Steinberg, *Acts of God: The Unnatural History of Natural Disaster in America* (New York: Oxford University Press, 2000), xvii. See also Cutter, *Hazards, Vulnerability, and Environmental Justice.*

6. "Jackson County Meeting Helped Offset Hurricane," *Biloxi-Gulfport Daily Herald*, August 27, 1969; Gary Pettus, "Devastating Hurricane Put Radio, TV Stations on Same Wavelength . . . Camille: Everyone Pitched In," *Jackson Clarion-Ledger*, August 17, 1997, 1F, 2F.

7. Senate Special Subcommittee on Disaster Relief of the Committee on Public Works, *Federal Response to Hurricane Camille (Part I)*, 91st congress, 2nd session, 637–711 especially; "Segregation Not Evident in Evacuation," *Biloxi-Gulfport Daily Herald*, August 25, 1969; Butler, "Surface Similarities," 224–25. In response to Camille—which hit portions of southern Louisiana too—six racially segregated shelters were established in Plaquemines Parish. See Kenneth C. Schneider, "Epidemiological Aspects of Hurricane Camille. Morbidity in the Hurricane Shelter Populations of Plaquemines Parish, Louisiana. Adapted from presentation at the Epidemiology Session Fifth Joint Meeting, Clinical and Commissioned Officers Association, Washington, D.C., April 3, 1970," accessed at www.rosyfinch.com/HurricaneCamille.html (October 9, 2009).

8. "County Schools Make No Changes in Desegregation," *Biloxi-Gulfport Daily Herald*, January 15, 1969, 2; "HEW Asks for Delay on Mixing," *Biloxi-Gulfport Daily Herald*, August 26, 1969. Several key decisions, most notably Judge John Minor Wilson's decision in the Fifth Circuit's Jefferson County School Board (1966) and the 1969 case *Alexander v. Holmes County Board of Education* (396 U.S. 1218) did a great deal to empower HEW and gave the department considerable judicial authority.

9. For a profound criticism of, and problems associated with, the *Brown v. Board of Education*'s 1954 use of the phrase, "all deliberate speed," see *Alexander v. Holmes County Board of Education*, Supreme

Court of the United States, October term 1969, September 5, 1969, 396 U.S. 1218.

10. Lee Bandy, "South's Chances for Strong Anti-desegregation Good," *Biloxi-Gulfport Daily-Herald*, August 7, 1969.

11. "Only Complying Schools to Get Rebuilding Aid," *Biloxi-Gulfport Daily Herald*, August 27, 1969, 1; "Some Schools to Miss Funds," *New Orleans Times-Picayune*, sec. 1, August 27, 1969, morning edition, 20. On segregationists's establishment of private schools, see Leon Panetta's remarks in Tom Littlewood, "School Aid Cutoff Review," *New Orleans Times-Picayune*, sec. 2, August 24, 1969, morning edition, 2. The relevant sections of Title VI are sections 1 and 2, which mandated nondiscrimination in federally assisted programs and tied it to questions of financial assistance and noncompliance. Civil Rights Act of 1964, 2 July 1964, 88th Congress, H.R. 7152.

12. "Parents, Thank Camille for Two-Week Delay," *Biloxi-Gulfport Daily Herald*, August 22, 1969.

13. "Only Complying Schools to Get Rebuilding Aid," 1.

14. "Mississippi Told to Hold Up Spending," *Biloxi-Gulfport Daily Herald*, August 19, 1969.

15. "Officials Ask Funds Restored," *Biloxi-Gulfport Daily Herald*, August 21, 1969.

16. "Only Complying Schools to Get Rebuilding Aid," 1; "Johnston Eyes School Damage," *New Orleans Times-Picayune*, sec. 1, August 28, 1969, morning edition, 18.

17. Bolton, *The Hardest Deal of All*, 130; Butler, "Surface Similarities," 230; Mason, *Beaches, Blood, and Ballots*, 176–78.

18. Butler, "Surface Similarities," 230.

19. Willard Edwards, "Stennis Works Out a Deal," *Chicago Tribune*, September 11, 1969, 18; Council on Foreign Relations, "The Missile Defense Debate, A-to-Z Encyclopedia of National Missile Defense," available at www.cfr.org/virtualbooks/reference/glossary/glossary_s_z.html, (accessed October 8, 2007).

20. Robert B. Semple Jr., "Nixon Pleased by Stay on Coast," *New York Times*, September 7, 1969, 44.

21. "Faster School Desegregation?" *New York Times*, August 28, 1969, 38.

22. "HEW Asks for Delay On Mixing," *Biloxi-Gulfport Daily Herald*, August 26, 1969; Edwards, "Stennis Works Out a Deal," 18; "Federal Judges Back Delaying School Mixing," *Biloxi-Gulfport Daily Herald*, August 27, 1969. Leon Panetta, HEW's civil rights director, made explicit the nature and extent of Stennis's pressure and its impact. See his address, "Watch Not What We Say But What We Do," page 2, 61st Annual Convention NAACP Cincinnati, Ohio, June 29–July 3, 1970, Papers of the NAACP: Group VI, Series A, Administrative File Cont., Annual Conventions Cont. (Supplement to Part 1, 1966–1970, Meetings of the Board of Directors, Records of Annual Conferences, Major Speeches and Special Reports), Reel 12. See also Panetta's detailed account of Stennis's involvement and Finch's awkward position in Panetta, *Bring Us Together*, 252–75.

23. "NASA Pledges Economy Lift to Gulf Coast," *New Orleans Times-Picayune*, sec. 1, August 30, 1969, morning edition, 1; Robert M. Smith, "Aid to Segregated Schools in Storm's Path Studied," *New York Times*, August 30, 1969, 22; Fred P. Graham, "Finch Asked to Explain School Integration Delay," *New York Times*, August 23, 1969, 15.

24. Edwards, "Stennis Works Out a Deal," 18. See George Lardner Jr., "Policy on Schools Defended by Finch," *Washington Post*, September 14, 1969, A8. I do not mean to minimize the significance of the delay. It was yet another postponement in a long struggle against racial injustice. See the apt criticisms in "Statement to Delegates and Branches Concerning Presidential Abandonment of New Guidelines," Association for the Advancement of Colored People, 60th Annual Convention, Jackson, Mississippi, June 29–July 5, 1969.

25. John Herbers, "H.E.W. to Demand Schools Act Now on Desegregation," *New York Times*, November 15, 1969, 1, 21; John Herbers, "Panetta's Ouster Linked to Policy," *New York Times*, February 19, 1970, 1, 36.

26. See Nathan Glazer, *Affirmative Discrimination: Ethnic Inequality and Public Policy* (New York: Basic Books, 1975), 80.

CHAPTER 3 The Political Economy of Disaster Recovery

The epigraph is from the "Voices of the Storm" issue of the *Southern Quarterly* 43 (Spring 2006): 129.

1. "In the Wake of Camille," *New Republic*, January 10, 1970, 8.

2. Jennie Jenevein interview, MOI, vol. 225, p. 30. For sensible commentary on why some people refused to evacuate—ranging from mixed messages concerning the severity of the storm to foolish complacency—see Kathleen R. Leyden, "Recovery and Reconstruction after Hurricane Camille: Post Storm Hazard Mitigation on the Mississippi Gulf Coast," National Science Foundation Report, Grant number CEE-9217115, August, 1985, 47–51.

3. "In the Wake of Camille," 8.

4. John Switzer interview, MOI, vol. 227, p. 18. More work needs to be done on how the banking industry functions and recovers in times of disaster. The Switzer interview is a good place to start for Camille not least because it shows how those banks that were hardest hit had to reconstruct individual bank accounts using microfilm. In instances where bank records had been destroyed by the hurricane—and several branch banks were, in Switzer's estimation, "almost totally destroyed"— the banks "would just have to give everybody credit for what they had." See vol. 227, p. 20.

5. According to one detailed study, relatively few homeowners had flood insurance. The National Insurance Program was still nascent, although some parts of the Disaster Relief Act of 1970 were made retroactive to August 1, 1970, in an effort to assist Camille's victims. See Leyden, "Recovery and Reconstruction after Hurricane Camille," 32–33.

6. *Time*, November 28, 1969, 99.

7. Lois Toomer interview, MOI, vol. 236, p. 63; Edith Byrd De Vries interview, MOI, vol. 201, pp. 43, 44; Jenevein interview, MOI, vol. 225, p. 19.

8. "In the Wake of Camille,"9. Some toyed with the idea of emigrating to Australia but ended up staying. Toomer interview, MOI, vol. 236, p. 64. Insurance companies certainly left. Only 85 companies remained on the Mississippi coast a year after Camille; beforehand, there were 280 companies. See "In the Wake of Camille," 8–9.

9. Gerald Peralta interview, MOI, vol. 224, p. 38.

10. "In the Wake of Camille," 8. The Red Cross loaned money too. Some people apparently gamed the system, borrowing money from the Red Cross, investing it in banks, and getting "quite a bit more interest [than they were paying]." De Vries interview, MOI, vol. 201, p. 41.

11. "In the Wake of Camille," 9. Many storm victims went to the Red Cross first, which quickly established twenty-nine emergency field offices. For the Mason quotation and the fractious history between black Mississippians and the Red Cross, see "NAACP Score Red Cross Bias," *The Crisis*, February, 1970, 61.

12. Switzer interview, MOI, vol. 227, pp. 21–22.

13. Peralta interview, MOI, vol. 224, p. 38; Jenevein interview, MOI, vol. 225, pp. 26–27. She then "went three times" to the Small Business Administration: "I never did get anything."

14. Dorothy Mae Demetz Niolet interview, MOI, vol. 226, p. 41.

15. Mr. and Mrs. Stegenga interview, MOI, vol. 201, p. 54; "In the Wake of Camille," 8.

16. "In the Wake of Camille," 8, 9; Dorothy Mae Demetz Noilet and Fred Demetz interview, MOI, vol. 226, p. 81.

17. Jenevein interview, MOI, vol. 225, p. 27. By the SBA's own account, they were slow to tackle the problem mainly because they used the aftermath of Hurricane Betsy (1965) as a guide. Camille's damage was much worse than Betsy's, and the SBA failed to appreciate the colossal scale of the damage wrought. See Tom Cook, "Camille Recovery Big Job for SBA," *Biloxi-Gulfport Daily Herald*, September 29, 1969, 15. For a comparison of Betsy to Camille, see Charles L. Sullivan, *Hurricanes of the Mississippi Gulf Coast* (Biloxi, Miss.: Gulf Publishing Co., 1986), 92–93.

18. Niolet interview, MOI, vol. 226, p. 41. See also Stegenga interview, MOI, vol. 201, p. 26.

19. "The Conference on Information and Psychological Aspects of a Major Disaster," October 24, 1972, McCain Library and Archives, University of Southern Mississippi. Mrs. Lois Toomer believed that "[m]any people had all kinds of medical and mental problems" after Camille, sometimes manifesting themselves years after the event. Toomer interview, MOI, vol. 236, p. 63.

20. Peralta interview, MOI, vol. 224, p. 44; Stegenga interview, MOI, vol. 201, p. 27.

21. "In the Wake of Camille," 9, 10.

22. Toomer interview, MOI, vol. 236, p. 63; Major Martha J. Leslie, "Hurricane Camille and Camp Shelby, August 17, 1969," Mississippi Nurses' Association, Box 17, Folder (Historical File Camille), p. 2, Mississippi Department of Archives and History, Jackson, Miss. (hereafter, MDAH) Another way to understand differential impact and recovery is through micro and highly local lenses. Different counties and specific areas within coastal counties recovered at different rates depending on, among other factors, the level of expertise of local municipal officials in securing their share of federal recovery funding, the time it took to recover lost municipal revenues, and the speed with which structures were rebuilt. These metrics are described in detail in Leyden, "Recovery and Reconstruction after Hurricane Camille," 30–36.

23. "In the Wake of Camille," 9; Combined Community Organizations Disaster Committee, "Draft Memo on Discrimination after storm," August 29, 1969, 2, Charles Horowitz Papers, Delta Ministry Records, Box 2, Folder 3, MDAH.

24. Observations and quotation from Kenneth C. Schneider, "Epidemiological Aspects of Hurricane Camille. Morbidity in the Hurricane Shelter Populations of Plaquemines Parish, Louisiana. Adapted from Presentation at the Epidemiology Session Fifth Joint Meeting, Clinical and Commissioned Officers Association, Washington, D.C., April 3, 1970," accessed at www.rosyfinch.com/HurricaneCamille.html. Given the appalling state of hospital services for African Americans in Mississippi generally, there is little reason to suspect that African Americans in southern Mississippi fared any better after Camille. See John J. MacAllister, *Hospital Facilities in Mississippi* (Business Research Station, Special Study Series bulletin, Number Eight, 1953), 17 esp. Skin injuries—in addition to a general increase in gastroenteritis (courtesy of contaminated food and water)—are a hallmark of hurricanes. Most lacerations occur during the clean-up phase. See Gloria Butler Baldwin, "Health Department Assessing Situation," *Jackson Clarion-Ledger*, September 30, 1998. See

also The American National Red Cross, "Hurricane Camille: Nursing and Medical Task Force Action," Mississippi Nurses' Association, Box 17, Folder 6, MDAH.

25. James Michael Butler, Jr., "Surface Similarities: A Comparative Analysis of Civil Rights Struggles in Harrison County, Mississippi, and Escambia County, Florida," Ph.D. diss., University of Mississippi, 2001, 230–33; Gilbert R. Mason (with James Patterson Smith), *Beaches, Blood, and Ballots: A Black Doctor's Civil Rights Struggle* (Jackson, Miss.: University Press of Mississippi, 2000), 176–78; James H. Downey, "Governor's Council Gets New Members," unidentified newspaper clipping dated Jan. 11 1970, Charles Horowitz Papers, Delta Ministry Reports, Box 2, Folder 30, MDAH; "Nixon's 'New Federalism' Is the Same Old Racism," media release by Robert G. Clark, December 2, 1969, Charles Horowitz Papers, Delta Ministry Reports, Box 2, Folder 4, MDAH.

26. Gerlach interview, MOI, vol. 178, p. 10.

27. Switzer interview, MOI, vol. 227, pp. 42–43.

28. "In the Wake of Camille," 9, 10.

29. "In the Wake of Camille," 9.

30. Disaster Unemployment Assistance in Mississippi, Dec. 15, 1969–Aug. 31, 1970, Mississippi Employment Security Commission, Jackson, Miss., Dec. 1970. See also, "Hurricane Has Effect on Area Labor Market," *Biloxi-Gulfport Daily Herald*, September 25, 1969.

31. "In the Wake of Camille," 8, 10.

32. "In the Wake of Camille," 8, 10; Leyden, "Recovery and Reconstruction after Hurricane Camille," 36–37. See also Butler, "Surface Similarities," 226–27.

33. "In the Wake of Camille," 8, 10.

34. "In the Wake of Camille," 10.

35. Of course, Mississippi's Gulf Coast casino industry emerged principally in the 1990s, after extensive debate and no little political wrangling. See Butler, "Surface Similarities," 248–50.

36. *Down South* 19, no. 6 (1970): 4–5; Emily Germanis, "Tourist Industry to Rebuild," *Biloxi-Gulfport Daily Herald,* September 17, 1969. See also the helpful analysis in Butler, "Surface Similarities," 235–38 esp.

37. The very structures of these new hotels and centers were designed to withstand another Camille. The Sheraton, for example, was being "erected with the strongest type of construction known." "The main convention facility," it was boasted, "is 40 feet above sea level" with piles driven "90 feet into the ground." Germanis, "Tourist Industry to Rebuild."

38. George Lammons, "Storm Blew Opportunity with Disaster," *Biloxi-Gulfport Sun Herald*, August 20, 1989.

39. Peter Baker and Campbell Roberston, "Obama Meets Critics in New Orleans," *New York Times*, October 15, 2009. On the continuing housing crisis in southern Mississippi, see Rick Jervis, "Many in Miss. Still Lack Homes after '05 Storms," *USA Today*, Friday September 25, 2009, 3A.

≈ ≋ ≋

Index

Peralta, Gerald, 12
Pyle, R. Wayne, 55n1

recovery and relief efforts: by
    CCODC, 44, 45; by federal gov-
    ernment, 26, 28–29, 30–35,
    41–43, 48, 49–51; by Hurricane
    Emergency Relief Council, 31,
    45; and insurance, 38–39, 63n5;
    long-term, 36–37, 41–43, 45,
    49–50, 51–53; race and class
    disparities in, 39–41, 43–48, 53,
    65n22; short-term, 36–41, 44,
    49, 51; and unemployment, 46,
    47–48; by voluntary associa-
    tions, 39. *See also* Department of
    Health, Education, and Welfare;
    Department of Housing and
    Urban Development; Office of
    Economic Opportunity; Red
    Cross; Salvation Army; Small
    Business Administration
Red Cross, 15–16, 39–41, 45, 53,
    64nn10–11
Robert E. Lee Hotel (Jackson, Miss.),
    27
Ryals, Herman W., 38

Safeguard missile system, 31–33
Salvation Army, 16, 39, 40, 41
segregation: and Camille, 23, 24,
    26–27, 28–35, 40, 43–45, 47, 60n7;
    and federal politics, 24–25, 26,
    27–35
senses: and Camille, 4–5; and his-
    torical inquiry, 5–7; and intersen-
    sorality, 6, 18–19; mastery of, 4–5,
    20; and modernity, 4–5, 6–7, 10,

12, 14–15, 16, 18, 19–20. *See also*
    individual senses
sight: and Camille, 7–13, 19; and
    certainty, 5, 6–7, 12; and cosmet-
    ics, 17
Small Business Administration
    (SBA), 42–43, 45, 46–47, 64n17
smell: of Camille, 5, 14–16; regula-
    tion of, 5; of spam, 15–16
sound: of Camille, 13–14, 17, 18–19;
    regulation of, 5
states' rights, 30, 51
Steinberg, Ted, 26
Stennis, John, 31–33, 34, 62n22
Strategic Arms Limitations Talks
    (SALT), 31
Sumner, Charles, 21–23, 35
Swetman, Chevis, 52, 53
Switzer, John, 45–46, 63n4
Symington, Stuart, 32

taste: and Camille, 14, 15–16; and
    modernity, 5
Tocqueville, Alexis de, 39
touch and hapticity: and Camille,
    16–18, 18–19; and segregation, 5,
    17–18; and skin-care industry, 16;
    and social conventions, 5

Watergate, 50
Waveland, Miss., 2
"We Care," 49
Whitten, Jamie L., 28
Williams, John Bell, 27, 31, 45, 48,
    49. *See also* Governor's Emergency
    Council

Zebrowski, Ernest, 55n1

CPSIA information can be obtained at www.ICGtesting.com
Printed in the USA
LVOW080855170512

282135LV00002B/13/P